Dear Eleanor
Happy Birthday

Living the Ancient Psalms

A Little something
to tell you "I Love You"
on Page 188 - something
I like very much...
Something new to Read
And think...
I will always Love You!
May 2018

Grand-Ma Lise Petit

Living the Ancient Psalms

MESSAGES FOR MODERN LIFE

Judith Galas

FALL RIVER PRESS

New York

FALL RIVER PRESS

New York

An Imprint of Sterling Publishing
1166 Avenue of the Americas
New York, NY 10036

ISBN 978-1-4351-5215-1

Distributed in Canada by Sterling Publishing
c/o Canadian Manda Group, 165 Dufferin Street
Toronto, Ontario, Canada M6K 3H6
Distributed in the United Kingdom by GMC Distribution Services
Castle Place, 166 High Street, Lewes, East Sussex, England BN7 1XU
Distributed in Australia by Capricorn Link (Australia) Pty. Ltd.
P.O. Box 704, Windsor, NSW 2756, Australia

For information about custom editions, special sales, and premium and corporate purchases, please contact Sterling Special Sales at 800-805-5489 or specialsales@sterlingpublishing.com.

Manufactured in China

2 4 6 8 10 9 7 5 3 1

www.sterlingpublishing.com

To Cindy,
who shares my journey

Contents

Lamentation

GOD, LIFE IS HARD

Supplication

GOD, PLEASE HELP ME

Praise

GOD, YOU ARE THE BEST

Thanksgiving

GOD, THANKS SO MUCH

Joy

GOD, LIFE IS A BLESSING

Acknowledgments

Sitting down each day to reflect and write on the psalms was itself a daily prayer practice, and I'm grateful to the unnamed poets who composed these poems thousands of years ago. Your works of faith resonated not only within your desert tribes, but also within me. Your poetry and love of God are ageless.

Inspiration, suggestions, and patience also came from many other sources. I'm indebted to Emily Elliott who found Robert Alter's *The Book of Psalms* at a garage sale and immediately knew it would have a home with me. The Rt. Rev. Dean Wolf's suggestion that I read *A Long Obedience in the Same Direction* by Eugene H. Peterson was valuable.

Others shared the psalms that moved them. Father Charles Polifka, who has prayed all the psalms thousands of times, guided me toward his four favorites: Psalm 141—"Lord…make haste to me"; Psalm 29 with its flashes of divine fire; Psalm 130—"Out of the depths I cry…"; and the joyous Psalm 150, which makes even bad days better.

Thanks to Heather Coates, for helpful quotes, to Jean Grant for her reflection and guidance on Psalm 12, to Lara West for revealing the blessings she's found in Psalm 121, and to the Rev. Barb Norris for thoughts on Psalm 41. Tim O'Brien's analysis of Psalm 90 led me to a deep appreciation for the human hunger to contribute something meaningful with our lives.

Thanks to Pastor Jennifer Keifer for sharing her love of Psalm 51 and for praying Psalm 47 specifically for me. The Rev. Josh Longbottom led me to Psalm 89 and its message of trusting in God even when we'd rather give up. Sara Wentz's love for both the despairing Psalm 137 and the healing Psalm 46—"Be still and know that I am God"—was a fitting reminder that the psalms are companions through life's pain and comforts.

Finally, to Cindy, whose love, patience, and support made this project of faith possible.

How to Use This Book

You can approach these reflections in several ways. As with any book, you can read this one from beginning to end, starting with the reflections in Lamentation and ending with those in Joy. This quick exploration will introduce you to the ideas and prepare you for a slower journey at another time.

You also might want to delve in either by following the topics that interest you or by selecting one of the five divisions that reflect your own mood.

The forty topics that appear throughout the book depict the people and issues everyone faces in modern life. Perhaps you'd like to explore how an idea like "noise" can spark a lament, a thanksgiving, or a joyous "Alleluia." Perhaps a topic strikes a particular chord in your life. For example, are distractions driving you crazy? Does news on terrorism and war unsettle you? Are you crazy in love with your family, friends, or relationships? Pursuing a topic thread might give you meaningful things to ponder.

Each of the book's five major divisions focuses on one of the overarching moods captured in the Psalter. When life felt hard or frightening, the ancient poets wrote laments and supplications either for themselves or for their nation. They wrote poems of praise and thanksgiving when they felt grateful for God's steadfast love and generosity. Sometimes, when a fusion of life and God brought an outpouring of jubilation, they simply sang for joy.

So, one way to approach this book would be to take your own emotional pulse and find those sections that reflect your mood or that offer a counterbalance. Perhaps reading a psalm of joy will help soften your angry edges, or meditating on a lament might help you to understand your own sorrow.

You might also try using the psalm verses in the manner of *Lectio Divina*, or "divine reading." This Christian practice of scripture reading began within the early monastic traditions. The monks viewed scripture not as something to be studied, but rather as a gateway to God. A slow, thoughtful encounter with a psalm verse may stir images and feelings in your heart. Meditate on those feelings and images, and on how the verse and short reflection touch on your days. Think about what pleases you in your life, what troubles you, and what you would like to cling to or change. As your own thoughts bubble up, blend them into a prayer that captures where you are in that moment.

You also might explore this book through your own favorite psalms. The directory shows you which psalms are included. If, for example, Psalm 23 is a favorite, you can locate its verses on six different pages and see how it might illuminate ideas on "time," "self-confidence," or "poverty." Any psalm verse may also whet your appetite for the complete psalm, which you can locate in any Bible.

The beauty of the psalms rests in their accessibility. They capture the human story in compact verses and short, easy-to-read poems that lay open the human heart. May they open yours.

Introduction

The Israelites called their Psalter *tehillim* or "song of praise." With poetry and music, they lifted their voices in supplication, asking God to hear them and to respond to their innermost fears and joys. The psalmists wrote with an eye on God and on life. While they specifically addressed God, they often left out the specifics. We're left to wonder whether the speaker is truly ill of a grave disease or simply sick at heart. Were his enemies the Assyrians, his turncoat friends, or his own guilty conscience? We don't know.

Perhaps because of this vagueness, the psalms enable us to enter these poems and to find ourselves within the Psalter's human drama. We are free to align our pain, our fears, and our joys with those felt by believers thousands of years ago. Like the Israelites, we want to believe in God's eternal promise to love and protect us forever, if we in turn agree to follow God's laws.

For the Israelites and for us, God's laws aren't always easy to keep. Life, then and now, comes with troubles—war, terrorism, theft, and poverty. Like our ancestors, we love our families and relationships, but they also test us. We dread aging and death, and we struggle with caring for our neighbor; we are beset by worries, and we fear for our safety. Three thousand years may separate us from our Israelite brethren, but our emotions, concerns, and failings are the same.

Certainly, the Israelites' desert life was hard, but too often our own world seems difficult to navigate. Life wears us out with too little time, too many things to juggle, and not enough sleep. A barrage of bad news from the twenty-four-hour cycle makes our world feel uncertain and overshadows our true blessings. No wonder we feel out of sorts.

The Psalter, beckoning from the ages, offers a balm: Come and join with the voices calling to God from the wilderness and find your spiritual footing. Let these songs from the desert remind you that God stands at your side, ready to hear your worries and to share your joys. No matter the stress or fears lurking in our modern wilderness, the psalms can lighten our hearts and refresh our spirits with praise and thanksgiving. The psalms summon us to the healing power of God.

Be still, and know that I am God:

Psalm 46:10, KJV

Lamentation

God, life is hard

Aging

The days of our years are threescore years and ten;
and if by reason of strength they be fourscore years,
yet is their strength labour and sorrow;
for it is soon cut off, and we fly away.

Psalm 90:10, KJV

The psalmist laments life's brevity—maybe just seventy years. Yet, does it matter, he asks, if we gain another ten? Likely, those years will be filled with the hard work and the pain of growing even older.

I don't look forward to growing old, God, but I certainly don't want the alternative of dying in my seventies or even my eighties. Why, that's barely enough time! Yet, do I want a struggling old age? If I live long enough, I'll attend too many funerals and bury countless friends and loved ones. I'll be alone, and my life will grow small. Even as much as I want a long life, it's hard to think about failing years filled with pain and troubles. When I fear the trials of aging, God, help me to remember that my old body also holds a spirit that, like a kite, is tethered to this earth and body for only a few decades. Then You will cut it free and say, "Fly home to me."

Many believe that Moses wrote Psalm 90, and it is said he lived to 120.

Death

My heart is smitten,
and withered like grass;
so that I forget to eat my bread.

Psalm 102:4, KJV

The psalmist aptly describes his song as "a prayer of the afflicted, when he is overwhelmed, and poureth out his complaint before the Lord." The Israelites knew affliction, and they knew God. They knew if they lifted their broken hearts to God, he would hear them and soothe his troubled children. Even when faced with death, they could call to God.

My heart is broken, God, and I cannot find the pieces, for death has robbed me of my loved one. Is it possible to lose someone who is the center of your life and still want to keep going? Like dry grass, my spirit is shriveling up, and I'm exhausted from crying. People try to comfort me, yet I feel empty and alone. They say, "Eat," and I can't. They say, "Get some rest," but I know that even if I slept for days, I would not feel rested. If I called out to You, God, would You hear me? Can You revive my withered spirit? Can You help me believe in tomorrow and in the possibility that my heart will heal?

The Book of Psalms is the hymnal of the Israelites.

Decisions

You drench its furrows.
You level its ridges.
You soften it with showers.
You bless it with a crop.

Psalm 65:10, WEB

As people of the desert, the Israelites knew what it meant to till thirsty ground. They sang their appreciation for the rains that helped the soil yield to their plows and that pointed to the possibility of a good harvest.

God, some decisions are just hard to make, but why do I have to make so many? Heck, some days I don't even want to decide what's for dinner. Lately, however, I face steady pressure to make too many important decisions, and I'm nervous. I know my decisions affect not only me, but they also impact others. I can feel my brow furrow with each new weight. Clearly, I suffer from a thinking drought, and my mind has hardened so that others' suggestions run off me like a gully washer over parched earth. God, let Your wisdom soak into me and help me to remember that I am not alone when I struggle with choices, because You stand ready to soften my fears and bless the fruit of my decisions.

The Israelites would have sung Psalm 65 as a communal prayer of thanksgiving for God's blessings.

Depression

They wandered in the wilderness in a desert way.
They found no city to live in.
Hungry and thirsty,
Their soul fainted in them.

Psalm 107:4–5, WEB

God delivered the Israelites from exile, and they sang in thanksgiving for their safe return to the Promised Land. They had lived without hope, slaves to their captors in a strange land, but God had not forgotten them.

These days I wander in sadness, for nothing brings me joy. What has kidnapped my spirit that I'm so surrounded by gloomy thoughts? Nothing appeals to me; even food has no taste. I thirst for some diversion, but I have no energy to leave my room or my home. I've heard about the wretched Hebrews. I know they too were despondent, but their story ended well—God delivered them. This melancholy holds me captive against my will. Will You deliver me, God? Will You free me from this depression? This time of exile is so hard on me. I need to believe that even during this deep sadness, You will lead me out of the darkness just as You lead the Israelites back into the Promised Land.

Some Bible scholars think Psalm 107 was written in thanksgiving after the Hebrews' return from exile.

Disappointment

I waited patiently for the Lord;
and he inclined unto me, and heard my cry.

Psalm 40:1, KJV

The psalmist opens with a song of praise. No matter God's power and magnificence, the creator of all will bend toward Earth and listen to his children's cries. This act of generosity from one so great brings a poem of adoration from the Hebrews. Be patient just a bit longer and trust, the poet reminds them.

It's so hard to be patient. I want the heartache to go away now. I want the sadness to vaporize this minute. When I pray and pray and nothing changes, I can't help but ask, "God, where are You? Why are You ignoring me?" Then I remember that patience is a part of prayer, and I wonder if I can endure even the waiting without Your help. Isn't it hard enough to face disappointment? Must I also be patient while I suffer through it? My world revolves around instant communication. If You can't answer me now, help me to imagine Your ear bent my way, getting ready to listen. Better yet, help me to picture Your fingers poised and ready to tweet. Please.

Bono and the Irish rock band U2 created a soulful rendition of Psalm 40 that can be found on YouTube.

Distractions

Be still before the Lord, and wait patiently for him;
do not fret over those who prosper in their way,
over those who carry out evil devices.

Psalm 37:7, NRSV

Don't let yourself be troubled by those who seem to be doing so much better than you are, the psalmist urges. Do not be fooled by falseness. Instead, follow the wisdom of God, and remember that those who obey God's laws will prosper.

Sometimes green is my most unattractive color—the green of envy. I often let others' good fortune distract me from making goodness happen in my own life. When I hear of someone's latest romance, or promotion, or exotic vacation, the news stops me cold. Why not me? When is it my turn to enjoy the good life? It's so hard not to feel like life is passing me by, while others are having an exceptional ride. Help me, God, to keep my focus on Your designs for me. Tune my ears to You, so I'm not distracted by others' tales of success. My heart should explore Your presence in my life and not forget to see and appreciate the many blessings You already have given me and to believe in the triumphs still to come.

The Hebrews experienced leprosy, so fret—"to eat away"—held a powerful reminder not to be eaten alive by anger.

Dreams

I said, O my God,
take me not away in the midst of my days:
thy years are throughout all generations.

Psalm 102:24, KJV

The Israelites linked long life to a blessed life, and to have a life cut short was a sign of God's displeasure. The psalmist pleads with God to be generous when allotting his time on Earth. After all, God knows the joy of an everlasting life. Surely, the psalmist argues, God could be generous with him.

Making dreams come true takes time, God, so please don't cut my life short before I've lived long enough to achieve my aspirations and to realize my dreams while surrounded by the people I love. What good will it do to work hard in my career, if my friends won't be around to congratulate me on my achievements? I want the house I've been planning in my head to happen while loved ones can sit around my table, romp in the backyard, and marvel at my good fortune. Repeatedly, You promised the Israelites a happy ending. If I am faithful to You, is it asking too much to let me taste my happy future?

The fifth of the Penitential Psalms, Psalm 102 carries this introduction: "The prayer of the afflicted when he is overwhelmed..."

Environment

The heavens declare the glory of God;
the skies proclaim the work of his hands.
Day after day they pour forth speech;
night after night they reveal knowledge.

Psalm 19:1–2, NIV

The night sky's grandeur has overpowered the psalmist, who hears within the earth's sparkling ceiling a silent but obvious proclamation: God is master of a great world. He knows that the silent heavens speak volumes about their creator.

I want to hear what the environment is telling me, but it seems like I need hearing aids or a way to tune out so many argumentative voices. Is our world in trouble from human carelessness? Is our thinning ozone and growing CO_2 numbers cause for alarm? Is politics clouding our judgment and preventing decision-makers from taking action? I don't know the science, but like the psalmist, I want to proclaim the obvious: God has given us a great creation. Can we just be watchful and let it share its knowledge? God, until the moment when my fellow humans get smarter, help me to look at Your creation as something that needs my care and concern and to see in this glorious gift Your ongoing love of me.

C.S. Lewis called Psalm 19 "the greatest poem in the Psalter and one of the greatest lyrics in the world."

Faith

Hear me, Lord, and answer me,
for I am poor and needy.
Guard my life, for I am faithful to you;
save your servant who trusts in you.
You are my God;

Psalm 86:1–2, NIV

Help me, God," the psalmist entreats. "Hear me." In spite of whatever difficulty besets him, the psalmist does not let his troubles overshadow his faithfulness to God. He confidently entrusts his life to his creator, fully counting on God not only to hear him, but also to come to his aid.

Life can be hard, and sometimes my life seems especially bumpy. That's why I'm counting on You to see me through whatever difficulties head my way. When my heart aches and my tears flow, I plan to come to You. When I'm unsure about what to do or ashamed of what I have done, I will call to You. I'm counting on You to stand fast with me, so please don't let me down. Even when my own faith should waver a bit, I need to trust that when I call out Your name, You will answer. I must trust in Your faithfulness, for I could not bear facing life's struggles without You.

Borrowing lines from sixteen other psalms and Exodus, Psalm 86 becomes its own unique "Prayer in Time of Distress."

Family

Why are you in despair, my soul?
Why are you disturbed within me?
Hope in God! For I shall still praise him,
the saving help of my countenance, and my God.

Psalm 42:11, WEB

The psalmist is deeply homesick. Perhaps enemies have captured him and he now lives in exile. What is certain is that he is out of his element, away from his routine of worship. His very soul is disquieted as he thinks of home.

I miss my family, God. It's so hard to be away from their faces and voices, and from my own routine when I am with them. It seems like I can't even enjoy my morning coffee without seeing their sleepy yawns and tousled hair. When we're together, I forget to pay attention to the details of their expressions. Yet, when I'm away, I squeeze my eyes shut trying to force their faces to pop into my mind and smile at me. Hearing their voices on my phone or seeing their pictures on Facebook helps, but not enough. Like the psalmist, I'm homesick for what I love. Comfort me, God, and reassure me that this time of separation will soon pass, and I will kiss those sweet cheeks again.

Psalm 42 is one of the Psalter's strongest laments and speaks to an ongoing thirst for God.

Friends

Reproach has broken my heart
and I am so sick.
And I looked for sympathy, but there was none,
And for comforters, but I found none.

Psalm 69:20, NASB

Clearly, the psalmist's friends have abandoned him. He is in trouble, and he feels as if he has no one to turn to, no one who will help him or even feel sorry for him. The very people he trusted to support him have disappeared. He is bereft, and in his sorrow, he turns to God.

People say they're your friends, and then, bingo, they aren't. When you need them, they're gone. I've trusted people with my deepest secrets only to have them turn around and blab them to others, even going so far as to post my personal life on their web pages. I'm embarrassed, but I'm also angry. Why would someone want to hurt me like that? Don't I deserve better than to be the butt of people's jokes? My feelings get hurt time and again, and still I foolishly hope that someone will reach out to me and make me feel welcome. God, it's hard to lose friends; it's even harder to keep looking for them and coming up empty. God, can I friend You?

Many list Psalm 69 as a Messianic Psalm, because it seems to refer to the betrayal and suffering of Jesus.

Happiness

My life is consumed by anguish
and my years by groaning;
my strength fails because of my affliction,
and my bones grow weak.

Psalm 31:10, NIV

The psalmist cries out to God. He's so unhappy, he's sick. He worries that his enemies will triumph over him and that he will be consumed by sorrow. He knows that only God can rescue him.

Sadness shrouds me and seeps into my bones. Those doctors on television announce that stress makes people ill, and I'm definitely stressed out. Can sickness be far behind? I agonize over money, I struggle to make the right decisions for my family, and I take my responsibilities seriously. I worry that I'm not doing enough, and my sadness deepens to gloom when I fear I'm not taking good care of the people and duties in my life. Like enemies, my worries gloat over me and suck away any happiness I might feel from small successes. Some days I don't even want to get out of bed. I want to be like the psalmist, God, and sing out my despair, knowing in my heart that You'll hear my song. Help me, God, to remember You are listening; You will not let stress devour my happiness.

Psalms of lament, like Psalm 31, are the most common types in the collection of psalms.

Health

Then they cry to Yahweh in their trouble,
he saves them out of their distresses.
He sends His word, and heals them,
and delivers them from their graves.

Psalm 107:19–20, WEB

The psalmist sings with confidence about God's unfailing love and support in times of captivity, sickness, and distress. The God of the Hebrews promises to heal them, body and soul, if only they will put their trust in him and stand faithful.

I feel weak, when I want to feel strong. I want energy, not fatigue. Is it the flu? Is it cancer? Please don't let it be cancer, for I'm not brave or resilient. A simple head cold may be all I can handle. I try to eat right, and I know I should exercise more. Surely my efforts should save me from the expense and hassle of doctors' visits and prescriptions. I know, God, I sound too much like a whining child, but I don't want to be sick—not now. You nurtured the Hebrews' bodies as well as quelled their fears. I need that nurture. You commanded the earth to obey You; surely my body will listen to its creator. Help me to put my trust in You and feel strong.

Psalm 107 is among the psalms that celebrate God's sovereignty over the natural world.

Home

He led them by a straight way
to a city where they could settle.
Let them give thanks to the Lord *for his unfailing love*
and his wonderful deeds for mankind,

Psalm 107:7–8, NIV

The Hebrews had reason to lament. Lost in the desert, imprisoned, ill, or tossed about at sea, they called to God for deliverance, and God's unfailing love rescued them.

God, I hate it under this roof. Home should be a place of refuge and comfort, but instead it's a place of discord and disorder. Nothing seems in place, including our love for each other. Each morning I face things that need washing—dishes and my own disappointment. Each night I go to bed with things undone—the grocery shopping and the "I'm sorry" I didn't remember to say. You settled the Hebrews in a new place, and I want to ask, "Why not me?" Still, I'm smart enough to know that love is essential to the success of any resettlement and that without love and forgiveness, my life will never feel reconciled, no matter where I live. I can fervently imagine an escape route, but the example of Your love prompts me to wonder if my real move shouldn't be to a more loving life under this roof.

Verse 8 is the refrain repeated after each of the four stanzas in this psalm's first section.

Loneliness

I am like a pelican of the wilderness.
I have become as an owl of the waste places.

Psalm 102:6, WEB

The psalmist's imagery captures his deep despair. Perhaps fearing he is near death, he describes himself as various solitary birds surviving in a bleak land. In other verses, he compares his heart to withered grass and his life to the ephemeral quality of smoke—barely visible and then gone. Desolation pervades his spirit.

Loneliness feels a little like dying. I'm alive, but I'm not living. I want to connect with others, but I feel so out of step with family and friends. Are their interests so different from my own or does it only seem that way? Perhaps I've brought this lonely life on myself. Sometimes I let work separate me from others. I told people I was too busy, and being busy made me feel important. Now it only makes me feel left out. God, I'm not sure what I did with all my days that I now find myself with empty time. I struggle to come up with a re-entry plan that makes me feel a part of the world. I want to step into life. Show me the door and help me open it.

With its stirring imagery, the entirety of Psalm 102 provides one of the Psalter's most compelling poems.

Money

And enter not into judgment with thy servant:
for in thy sight shall no man living be justified.

Psalm 143:2, KJV

The psalmist finds himself trapped in an uncomfortable debate. At first, he takes the more depressing, but logical, side. No one can escape God's judgment and come out well, for no one is without blemish. Therefore, no sinner can hope to justify himself to God. On the other hand, the psalmist hopes he can fall back on God's mercy, the gift that steadfastly has sustained him and his fellow Israelites.

I wish that thinking about money—who has it and who doesn't—didn't make me feel so shallow. I know that judging people by how much money I think they make or have in the bank is superficial, even unkind; but too often, I find myself scrutinizing others based on dollar signs. I find myself wondering if a well-dressed person has money or pretense. I watch an expensively bejeweled hand reach for the collection plate, and I ponder if the person contributes enough. If someone with a good salary suggests we go Dutch treat, I wonder why he's being cheap. Only You know the generosity or stinginess in someone's heart, so why is it so hard for me to remember that You are arbiter, not me?

Early Christians believed that King David wrote all the psalms, inspired by God and his own personal trials.

Nature

Yahweh, how many are your works!
In wisdom have you made them all.
The earth is full of your riches.

Psalm 104:24, WEB

The Israelites wandered frightened, homeless, and hungry and thirsty in the desert. They cried to God to spare them, because beyond their fear and discomfort was their faith in the creator's power and design. The land not only frightened them, but it also fed and sustained them. In its harsh beauty, they found God.

God, sometimes Your creation terrifies me. Hurricanes howl, and the earth rocks buildings into rubble. Floods devour crops, possessions, and people, even as droughts bring famine. Invisible microbes and viruses trigger disease and suffering. We feel at the mercy of nature. Too small to fight back, we often find ourselves caught by surprise and unprepared for the vagaries of Your creation. Like the Israelites wandering in the desert, we cry to You to spare us, and like the Israelites, we too must have faith in Your great design. When the earth stuns us with its beauty and nurtures us with its bounty, we trust entirely in Your wisdom. So must we trust Your creation, even when we do not understand its power.

The psalmist who wrote Psalm 104 reworked the story of creation into poetry.

Neighbor

If You, Lord, should mark iniquities,
O Lord, who could stand?
But there is forgiveness with You,
That You may be feared.

Psalm 130:3–4, NASB

As they walked up the hillside to the temple, the Israelites sang out their prayers to God. They knew they and their neighbors were sinners, but they willingly approached God, knowing that God forgave all no matter what they had done. Neither shame nor guilt could keep the faithful from calling out God's name.

I'm a rumormonger. I hate that about myself, yet when I have the chance to share a juicy tidbit about someone, I can't resist trying to be the center of attention by making someone else the center of my gossiping. It's hard to admit that I can be so callous about my neighbor's feelings and good name, whether that person lives down the street or works in a cubicle on my office floor. I picture myself standing before You repeating the rumors I've spread about others, and I'm ashamed. Guilt consumes me. The Israelites counted on Your forgiveness, and so I carry hope that You will find a way to let me know You forgive me.

Psalm 130, known as the *De Profundis* ("from the depths"), is prayed for the departed in Roman Catholic liturgy.

Networking

Behold, he travails with iniquity.
Yes, he has conceived mischief,
and brought forth falsehood.

Psalm 7:14, WEB

The psalmist knows someone has been spreading lies about him. While the falsehoods anger him and make him concerned for his reputation, he takes comfort in two things. He knows that God will judge him wisely on the quality of his life. He also knows that evil begets evil, and those who sought to ruin him will find themselves in jeopardy.

I admit it—social media is fun. I love getting the informal family pics and news about friends I thought I'd lost. Still, I shudder when networking turns ugly and advances the lies folks spread about others. Just today, I read of another teen who chose death rather than endure another moment of falsehoods careening her way from people's Facebook pages or tweets. God, our hearts are so vulnerable to the mischief of others, and our kids are especially fragile. Where can they find courage to stand up against meanness? How can we help them understand that they matter much more than the lies? God, it's hard to coexist with networks that make us laugh one moment and then shudder when they wreak havoc with people's lives.

Psalm 7 likely refers to when King Saul ruled and his friends spread lies about David, whom Saul disliked.

Noise

Then they cry to Yahweh in their trouble,
and he brings them out of their distress.
He makes the storm a calm,
so that its waves are still.
Then they are glad because it is calm,
so he brings them to their desired haven.

Psalm 107:28–30, WEB

The psalmist knows that when people feel in danger or suffer under a stressful burden, they can feel as if they are tossed about in a great sea. Unable to get their emotional footing and afraid that life's troubles will drown them, they call out to God, who answers them.

Noise engulfs me, and pandemonium permeates my life. Cell phones tone, computers ding, horns honk, timers beep, grown-ups whine, and children cry. Inside I yearn for simple peace and quiet. It seems like everyone and everything competes for my ears, and I can barely hear and respond to one conversation, much less the cacophony of voices and sounds in my life. I know life's noises will not disappear, but You can quiet my exasperation by helping me to open myself to Your calming presence. In the midst of the yammering, I have only to call quietly for You, and Your presence will enfold me and give me peace.

Psalm 107 emerged from the Israelites' gratitude that God delivered them from exile and returned them to their homeland.

People

I will lift up my eyes to the hills.
Where does my help come from?
My help comes from Yahweh,
who made heaven and earth.

Psalm 121:1–2, WEB

In their treks to celebrate the holy festivals in the temple, the Hebrews walked through unfamiliar lands. Together they would sing the psalms as they ascended toward Zion, encouraging each other in their bravery, their endurance, and their eagerness for a safe arrival.

I'm on a pilgrimage, God, toward finding a kinder and more open heart. I want to celebrate others and not be envious of those who seem to have it all. I know that jealousy stands in the way of my giving people sincere compliments. I fear my forced smile won't hide my keen desire to look as good or dress as well as the people I envy. I know that greediness keeps me from telling people I'm truly happy for their success. Instead, the smallness in my heart whimpers, "Why can't I have what they have?" God, are all these people part of Your plan to test me on my life's journey? If so, I'm too often failing those hard tests, even as I lift my thoughts to You for help to be better.

A Song of Ascent, Psalm 121 likely was sung at the start of the pilgrimage as a prayer of protection.

Popularity

For I have heard the slander of many:
fear was on every side:
while they took counsel together against me,
they devised to take away my life.
But I trusted in thee, O Lord: I said, Thou art my God.

Psalm 31:13–14, KJV

The psalmist, like the prophet Jeremiah, struggled with false friends and brutal enemies (Jer 20:10). In a land plagued by foes, it's no wonder the Hebrews grew mistrustful and afraid. Like Jeremiah, they had to remember to put their trust in God.

Nobody likes me; I can feel it. I try to make friends, but I just don't seem to fit in. I know it's silly to want to be popular. I know I'm not a teenager, but who doesn't want to believe that other people think they're great? Am I imagining it or are people gossiping behind my back? Am I not wearing the right clothes or saying the right things? I feel trapped, because I know I shouldn't care so much, and yet I do. God, it's hard to ignore these slights. Give me the wisdom to keep my ears tuned to You and not to the petty whispers of others. Help me to remember that when others fail me, I can put my trust in You.

These verses show the common shift in psalms of lament from profound distress to deep faith in God's saving power.

Poverty

You evildoers frustrate the plans of the poor,
but the Lord is their refuge.

Psalm 14:6, NIV

The poor were numerous among the Hebrews, so the psalmist reminds his listeners to follow God's wishes and to be mindful of the poor. Do not let others shame them or abuse them, and remember to be generous in helping those who have so little. Those who come to their aid will be paid richly in God's love.

Lord, I struggle with knowing that so many people live without the basics. The poor do not deserve hunger pangs, sidewalks for pillows, and rags for coats. They need softened hearts and faces willing to gaze into their eyes and see them for the human beings that they are. On the streets in my city, I see poor and struggling people, and I see those who ignore them or mock them. I grieve for those who have so little, but most often, I feel so helpless when faced with such want. I know that You are the refuge for the poor, but that doesn't help me to cope with what I see around me. Teach me how to ease such suffering. I'm listening for Your word.

Some psalms are close copies of others in the Psalter. There is a close copy of Psalm 14 in Psalm 53.

Relationships

Don't harden your heart, as at Meribah,
as in the day of Massah in the wilderness,

Psalm 95:8, WEB

The psalmist implores his people not to test their God. He urges them to remember when their ancestors wandered in the desert and murmured their impatience to God and Moses. The places of Meribah and Massah—Dispute and Testing—poignantly remind the Hebrews of a time of disobedience to a God who had delivered them from slavery.

I admit it; I'm hard-hearted. I'm unwilling to forgive people just because they give me sad eyes and say, "I'm sorry." I want them not to act like jerks in the first place, or just to do what's expected. Sure, I want good relationships with folks, but I feel like I'm always bending to what others want. Why do I have to wait patiently until others come around to my viewpoint? God, I know the Moses story. I know the Israelites were crabby with You and gave Moses a hard time, but they were tired, and thirsty, and afraid they were lost. Sometimes life's just hard. Sometimes people just expect too much. So, God, help me figure out whether I'm misunderstood or whether I might possibly not be that understanding.

Exodus 17:2–7 recounts the desert story, and in Hebrews 7–19, Christians are exhorted not to imitate their ancestors' disobedience.

Retirement

Cause me to hear your loving kindness in the morning,
for I trust in you.
Cause me to know the way in which I should walk,
for I lift up my soul to you.

Psalm 143:8, WEB

The poet wants to rise each morning to the sound of God's voice. Because he trusts in God's love, he awaits God's directions on how to live his life so that each day pleases him and God.

Some see retirement as the start of the next phase of life, but I fear it's the end to the career I worked so hard to build. Working for wages makes me feel like I matter. I have rank and position and a steady income. Retirement seems to signal that I am old and will have less money. I can't shake the feeling that when retirement comes, some things are off the table—an adventurous vacation or a flashy car that's too impractical for someone on social security. I hear others gleefully anticipating their last days on the job, but I'm afraid I'm going to lose something—my identity. I'd feel better, God, if You shared Your plans for my retirement.

Psalm 143 is one of the seven penitential psalms that ask God for forgiveness and guidance.

Safety

From the end of the earth will I cry unto thee,
when my heart is overwhelmed:
lead me to the rock that is higher than I.
For thou hast been a shelter for me,

Psalm 61:2–3a, KJV

Remembering that God has sheltered him in the past, the poet once again brings his petition to God. He seeks security, perhaps from enemies or perhaps from life's uncertainties. Maybe he was taken captive and lives in exile far from the temple in Jerusalem. He imagines his spiritual home—his rock and refuge.

Life doesn't come with safety nets, and that's a shame, because I'd like some guaranteed security in my life. Television ads assure me this investment company is sound, but is my money safe or should I invest with another firm? If I build my house on a hillside in the beauty of a forest or near the roar of the seashore, will a fire consume it or will mudslides or sea foam wash it and me away? I can see grim possibilities lurking within every life decision. An uncertain future overwhelms me at times, and I need help remembering that You have promised to shelter me. Point me in the direction of that solid ground, because I want to stand there with You.

Many psalms, including Psalm 61, included directions for a stringed instrument, like David's lyre, to accompany the singer.

Self-confidence

Turn to me, and have mercy on me,
for I am desolate and afflicted.

Psalm 25:16, WEB

The psalmist calls out his personal prayer: God, see me and have mercy on me. He knows his own transgressions have made him feel detached from God and miserable. The poet does not reveal how he lost his link to God. Instead, he reveals a trust that enables him to believe that his merciful God will forgive him, answer his plea, and put his troubled heart at peace.

Self-confidence isn't something you get and decide to tuck away for safe keeping like a gift certificate. I've learned that self-confidence clearly is something you can lose. It can slip out of you like a quarter through the hole in your pocket. Angry words and cutting criticisms helped to steal mine. Fear and tears made me doubt my strengths. I've been so insecure, that I never even noticed when I stopped looking people in the eye. I don't want to spend life looking at the ground. I don't want to freeze in fear of others' judgments. Help me to remember that You are my only judge and that You are the rock waiting to hold me up.

The Psalter captures a thousand years of the Israelites' struggles and their ongoing confidence in God.

Setbacks

He lifted me out of the slimy pit,
out of the mud and mire;
he set my feet on a rock
and gave me a firm place to stand.

Psalm 40:2, NIV

For the Hebrews, God stood ready to rescue those who had gone astray and to set them firmly on the right path. For this steadfast devotion, the psalmist and all present in the temple sang praises to God.

I'm bogged down. Things didn't go my way, and I can't keep my brain from spinning with "if only" or "what if." Why can't I push past dwelling on the wrong decision or the bad choice? Why can't I stop obsessing about the disappointments? In my personal tar pit, I'm trapped by thoughts of failure—a missed objective, a bad score, a lost opportunity. I want to scream, "I'll never get anywhere." God, at times like this, help me to remember that I'll stay stuck in Setback Mode if I don't turn to You. I need reminding that You can lift me out of the mire and put me down on firm ground. Only then will I once again move forward and taste success.

Verse 2 echoes Jeremiah 38:6 when King Zedekiah lowered the prophet into a cistern where he sank into the mire.

Sexuality

You have removed lover and friend far from me;
My acquaintances are in darkness.

Psalm 88:18, NASB

The psalmist sings the saddest of psalms. Perhaps he is ill and near death, or maybe he's a sinner who feels a gulf between himself and God. He might be someone whose friends or lover have abandoned him, because he has committed some crime or has been disfigured by injury or disease. In his isolation and pain, he lets loose his anger and cries, "Why, God? Why me?"

I can't sleep in an empty bed; I can't roll over and not find my love near me. I root in the pillows, hoping to catch some lingering sweet scent, but the sheets are cold, and I am alone. We have broken up, and warmth and comfort have deserted me. Was I the foolish one who said, "Good-bye"? Was that the last word hurled at me as the door slammed shut? I only know my body aches for tender caresses in familiar places. God, I believed that You meant for us to be partnered, so I will not feel shame to say I want my lover back. I am heartbroken, and my only comfort comes from believing You hear me and You care.

A leper, who would have endured socially enforced isolation, may have written Psalm 88, a song of heartbreak.

Sleep

I am like a desert owl,
like an owl among the ruins.
I stay awake;
I am like a solitary bird on a roof.

Psalm 102:6–7, HCSB

The psalmist is miserable and as forlorn as that solitary bird roosting above his head. Perhaps he is ill or maybe just troubled by worries that keep him awake. In his affliction, he calls out to God, whom he trusts to help him.

God, I have to get some sleep, but my body feels too restless and my mind busies itself with rehashing the day. What's gnawing at me so that sleep seems impossible? Sleep deprived, I drag myself through one exhausting day after another, only to toss and turn at night while I listen to others in my house snore. My bedroom once was a place of relaxation, now I dread facing this nightly struggle to find my "Off" button. I'm hot, then I'm cold. The bed's too hard, then too soft. As I watch the clock tick away the hours, I fret that I have fewer and fewer hours to nod off. God, You are a refreshment in my life, a source of renewal. Help me stop this restlessness and feel restored. Give Your insomniac a good night's sleep.

The Psalter is divided into five books, which might reflect the Pentateuch, the opening five books of the Old Testament.

Solitude

Give us help against the adversary,
for the help of man is vain.
Through God we shall do valiantly,
for it is he who will tread down our adversaries.

Psalm 60:11–12, WEB

When facing the enemies from without or within, the psalmist knows that it is foolish to rely on mere humans to save the day. An army that does not include God in its ranks will not taste victory. Citizens who do not involve God in their conversations will struggle with discord. Strife is a common adversary, but the person who struggles without God struggles in vain.

I am my greatest enemy. I yearn for some quiet time, yet I fill up my calendar until I barely have time to sit down, much less think about anything but the next highlighted item on my list. When someone asks, "How have you been?" I blurt out, "I've been so busy." Busyness has become my badge of honor and my enemy. If I want time for myself, I clearly can't rely on others to give it to me. In truth, I can't seem to give it to myself, and I'm the keeper of my calendar. God, help me to figure out how to stop sabotaging my own need for solitude.

Psalm 60 reflects on past and future conquests, and laments Israel's losses against common enemies—Philistines, Edomites, Moabites, and Syrians.

Strangers

For I am poor and needy,
and my heart is wounded within me.
I am gone like the shadow when it declineth:
I am tossed up and down as the locust.

Psalm 109:22–23, KJV

The poet drapes himself in sorrow and affliction. His enemies have sorely mistreated him, and earlier he cursed them and prayed that they and their families would come to harm. Now, softened but still distressed, he brings his bitterness to God. While others brush him away like a locust clinging to cloth, God will embrace him and ease his pain.

I'm tired of enduring one occasion after another when I feel like the new kid in town—new on the job, the strange face in the neighborhood, or the outsider in the break room where everyone but me has something to say. I hate feeling like a stranger, but I hate it even more when it feels as if people try to exclude me. Would it kill someone to say, "Hi"? Maybe they should see how it feels to be in my uneasy shoes, waiting for someone to make eye contact or smile. Am I being too sensitive, God? It's hard to sense the social chill, but even harder for me to break the ice.

An individual lament, Psalm 109 is an imprecatory psalm, a poem that curses or wishes harm to the poet's enemies.

Strength

Let the words of my mouth, and the meditation of my heart,
be acceptable in thy sight,
O Lord, my strength, and my redeemer.

Psalm 19:14, KJV

The whole of Psalm 19 touches upon essential elements in the Israelites' faith. God's creation speaks of his glory, and God's laws are the necessary and satisfying guideposts of life. In this closing verse, the psalmist offers a hopefulness that the Hebrews will prove themselves worthy of their great and deserving God. In fourteen poetic verses, he captures all that could ever matter to him and to Israel.

The Israelites drew their strength from You, but I confess that too often it's hard for me to remember Your instructions while I live my life. Social pressures tell me that a sign of strength is a ripped body sporting washboard abs, but I know that's not what You ask of me. You ask me for a different strength. You ask me to stand up for what's right, but also to know when it's time to stand down, to not fight, to not be mouthy with others. Being strong and staying strong in my faith in You is not easy. Some days I just need to know You see my struggles.

Verse 14 appears in Christian services as an invocation, and in Judaism, it concludes the period of silent meditation.

Terrorism

I went about mourning
as though for my friend or brother.
I bowed my head in grief
as though weeping for my mother.

Psalm 35:14, NIV

The psalmist has adversaries or at least people he does not like or trust. Nevertheless, when troubles beset his persecutors, he feels sympathy for them. He even behaves like a mourner, looking sad and crying for the tribulations of others. He knows that God values the man whose heart is so generous that he can feel compassion even for an enemy.

I'm angry that *jihadists* have left thousands maimed or dead in battlegrounds of the Middle East and Afghanistan. I'm incensed that terrorists throw acid at young girls' faces or strap bombs to their chests and walk into a crowded marketplace. God, this is madness. In spite of this insanity, help me to listen for Your word and to be guided by Your spirit. In war-torn lands, the innocent die and suffer. Mothers weep for children obliterated by the bombs they wore. Children cry for parents who had only gone to market and for sisters who had only gone to school. When my heart feels anger toward my enemy, let it soften in prayers for those who also suffer.

Some date Psalm 35 to David, either when Saul sought to kill David or when David's son Absalom battled him.

Theft

Unrighteous witnesses rise up.
They ask me about things that I don't know about.
They reward me evil for good,
to the bereaving of my soul.

Psalm 35:11–12, WEB

Like enemies everywhere, the psalmist's foes are wicked and unkind. God, defend me from such adversaries, he pleads. Stand by me in my time of need, for they are filled with lies and trickery. Surely, God will stand with the just and defend the innocent.

God, I can't believe people steal from each other. I don't have much, but just the thought of thieves helping themselves to my wallet, my car, or my good name makes me feel violated and tricked. It's not that I'm stingy about my things. I believe in people being generous with others, but I don't want to be victimized by people out for their own greed. I hate that my fear of unknown foes has me locking all my doors, hiding my paltry valuables in the trunk of my car, and mistrusting approaching strangers. Still I fret. Help me to remember, God, that You stand with the just. I'd like to imagine You standing right outside my door tonight.

Some find in David's lament of betrayal, the plight of Jesus when others reviled him in his last hours.

Time

He makes me lie down in green pastures.
He leads me beside still waters.

Psalm 23:2, WEB

The attentive shepherd leads his flock to lush grass and cool water. The psalmist, having watched those faithful shepherds many times, maybe even having been one, knows that nature's meadows and burbling streams refresh the spirit as well as the body. He also knows that shepherds are ever mindful of their sheep.

Life pulls in a thousand directions, and I'm a stringed puppet with my attention being jerked every which way and my time bled out of me until I feel like dry wood. Family, the job, my church, and my friends all want a piece of me. "Come with us." "Please do this." "Let's go there." Where's time for me? I dole out hours to others, and I barely ration precious minutes for myself. I yearn for respite. Shepherd of mine, lead me to a tranquil place now and then, and if I'm too busy and pay You no mind, please take Your crook and pull me in the right direction toward time with myself and with You.

On 9/11, Todd Beamer, a passenger on Flight 93, recited Psalm 23 before the plane crashed near Shanksville, Pennsylvania.

Violence

Yahweh, I love the habitation of your house,
the place where your glory dwells.
Don't gather my soul with sinners,
nor my life with bloodthirsty men;

Psalm 26:8–9, WEB

The psalmist, possibly King David, entreats God to see him among the righteous followers of God's law. Confident that he has tried to live a good and godly life, the singer puts his hope in God's mercy.

God, sometimes my anger rises up and I feel like striking out against others. I know You did not give me a voice to yell and curse at people. You did not give me hands so that I could hit and push others. Still, I confess to having too quick a temper; I fear that violence bubbles deep within and that I will erupt. Family members, the pokey driver ahead of me, people at work who make mistakes, and annoying strangers may be fair game for my rage. I don't know what makes me so furious, but I'm pleading with You to sow peace in my mind and healing in my heart. I do not want You to count me in the company of cruel and vengeful people.

Verse 9 is among those a priest says when washing his hands before the sacrificial moment in the mass.

War

Daughter Babylon, doomed to destruction,
happy is the one who pays you back
what you have done to us.
Happy is he who takes your little ones
and dashes them against the rocks.

Psalm 137:8–9, HCSB

The psalmist bitterly laments the destruction of Jerusalem, the captives' trek to Babylon, and the gleeful faces of their captors and destroyers. Having suffered from the exile, revenge bubbles up from the poet's heart. He wants his enemies to suffer as they made the Israelites suffer.

The psalmist's lament chills me, God, for it reminds me that even thousands of years ago, Your children turned from Your instructions to love each other and instead lusted for retaliation. My heart aches to be reminded that the sounds of war include the wails of mothers crying for their dead children and the cries of frightened children who have lost their parents, perhaps forever. At this moment somewhere, mothers and children cry, men grimace in pain or grieve for comrades, and citizens look in horror at the rubble that was once their city. God, I beg You, please help Your children to understand that vengeance and hatred doom us all to endless sorrow.

Psalm 137 was written during the Babylonian Exile, from which the Israelites did not return until 537 BCE.

Work

Yahweh looks from heaven.
He sees all the sons of men.
he who fashions all of their hearts;
and he considers all of their works.

Psalm 33:13, 15, WEB

The psalmist sings of God looking down on creation; and from heaven, he observes not just the Israelites, but also every person on Earth. Not only does he see them all, but he also peers deeply into their hearts and draws a full picture of each, body and soul.

I often chide myself for not achieving more, but I'm trying to work hard. I really am. Sometimes I wonder if others see my true effort. When they size up my achievements, do they think I'm a slacker because others seem to work harder than I do? I want others to see that I'm doing my best. I don't want them to be disappointed. When I have such worries, I turn my thoughts to You. I need reminders that You see all of me, the whole package, inside and out. You know my motives, my goals, and my energy level, and You know my insecurities. I need some reassurance that when You look at my whole person, You are pleased and might even think, "Good job."

As a song of creation, Psalm 33 is among the prayers Jews recite on Sabbath morning.

Worry

Have mercy upon me, O Lord; for I am weak:
O Lord, heal me; for my bones are vexed.
My soul is also sore vexed:
but thou, O Lord, how long?

Psalm 6:2–3, KJV

The psalmist feels as if God has abandoned him, or at least has turned a deaf ear. In his misery, he wonders if God has punished him with illness. In his lament, he asks how long God will stay silent, and he agonizes that God may not return to heal or help him.

People tell me to relax or lighten up, but their words are cheap and my worries are real. When things don't go well, I wonder if I am being punished for something I did or didn't do. I want to pray, and sometimes I pray fervently, but I'm never sure if You hear me. When things don't right themselves, I'm convinced You didn't hear a word I said. Even worse, I fear that You just ignored me. It's impossible to live worry free, so I need to believe that You have the power to smooth out the bumps in my life. Speak up, God. I want to hear You. Reach toward me; I need to feel Your presence.

Charles Spurgeon, the "prince of preachers," noted that John Calvin's favorite exclamation was, "*Domine usquequo,*" "O Lord, how long?"

Supplication

God, please help me

Aging

God, you have taught me from my youth.
Yes, even when I am old and gray-haired,
God, don't forsake me,
until I have declared your strength to the next generation,
your might to everyone who is to come.

Psalm 71:17a, 18, WEB

The aging psalmist entreats God not to forget him now that he is old, but he isn't worried. He knows God has stood by him since his youth and will not desert him on the last leg of his journey. He also knows he has a few more lessons to teach the younger generation.

God, the elders in my life are fading away—auburn hair to silver, broad shoulders and straight backs to rounded ones. I kiss their wrinkled cheeks, smooth their thinning hair. I look into eyes that are a bit cloudier and gently grasp hands with turning fingers and paper-thin skin. I need to believe that you have not forsaken them, that you stand by their walkers and lift chairs. You watch over them in nursing homes, hospital rooms, and houses now quiet after years of bustle. Help me to feel confident that You are near when I cannot be and to remember that I must treasure their conversations, for in their voices I will hear of Your truths.

Some Bible scholars think an aging King David wrote Psalm 71 to reflect on God's presence throughout his life.

Death

Let my prayer enter into your presence.
Turn your ear to my cry.
For my soul is full of troubles.
My life draws near to Sheol.

Psalm 88:2–3, WEB

The Hebrews believed when they died they went to Sheol, the shadowy underworld, and within Sheol was the pit, the deepest and darkest region. The psalmist knows he is dying. He is anxious and sad. Still, he lifts a prayer to God, whom he fears has abandoned him at his bleakest hour.

God, death terrifies me. Sometimes before I fall asleep, I panic: What if I don't wake up? I fight the blankets as I struggle with thoughts of my world without me in it. Too often I imagine death's presence and recoil. A car swerves into my lane, and I imagine mangled metal and hear the wail of sirens. I fly through turbulence and think, "This is it!" as I grip the armrest, ready to plummet to earth. I dread doctor visits, because surely I'll learn something frightening. God, help me to embrace today and to stop imagining some gruesome ending. Help me to focus on living rather than dying. Remind me that You are near, so that the fear of death loosens its grip on my heart.

Many consider Psalm 88 the most despondent of the psalms, for the poet sings a most bitter lament.

Decisions

Why do you stand far off, Yahweh?
Why do you hide yourself in times of trouble?
Arise, Yahweh! God, lift up your hand!
Don't forget the helpless.

Psalm 10:1, 12, WEB

The psalmist knows the Israelites have experienced struggle, disappointment, and even doubt. In times of trouble, they lifted their voices to God, even when they worried about whether God was listening. In the end, they decided to put their trust in God.

God, I've got some important decisions to make. My friends have poor judgment, and I suffer the fallout. They gossip about each other and then expect me to join the negativity. They spend their own money and then ask to borrow mine, and I know I won't see a dime in repayment. When their hearts get broken in unwise flirtations, they want to cry on my shoulder, but whose shoulder do I have? Either I need to set some firm boundaries with people who take advantage of me or I need to form friendships with people who treat each other with more respect. Both decisions are hard for me. I don't want to hurt anyone, but I want to protect myself from others' bad choices. God, I have decided to turn to You. Are You listening?

The psalms are religious lyric poetry written in the poetic style of "free verse," with no rhyming.

Depression

The troubles of my heart are enlarged.
Oh bring me out of my distresses.

Psalm 25:17, WEB

The psalmist turns to God in his distress. If he has enemies, God will protect him. No matter who turns away from him, God will embrace him. If shame or remorse burdens him, God will forgive. Clearly, the psalmist finds comfort in knowing God is near and listening.

It's bad enough when the blues grip me, but it's so much harder to see friends and loved ones disappear into their own despondency. I hear so much talk about the rising suicide rates, especially among young people, and I fear for the folks in my life. So, I try to cheer them up, but often it seems that my jollity only makes them withdraw even more. God, it's hard to be a bystander to someone else's sorrows. You watched the Israelites suffer, You heard their pleas, and You remained steadfast. Is that the answer? If I'm a good listener and remain a comforting presence in their lives, will I ease their distress? The psalmist gives me a glimmer of hope, because he reminds me that a listening ear and a warm embrace can guide a burdened heart to safer ground.

Psalm 25 is one of nine alphabet or acrostic psalms that use the Hebrew alphabet to aid in remembering the verses.

Disappointment

Uphold me according to your word, that I may live.
Let me not be ashamed of my hope.

Psalm 119:116, WEB

The Israelites faced disappointments many times—in the desert, in captivity, and against conquering foes. In moments of suffering or uncertainty, they turned to God's words for guidance. In God's decrees, they found the reassurance that they were doing what was right even in troubling times.

God, when I read the Bible or listen to the Gospel, I hear Your words. They hold out the promise that Your love is forever and Your forgiveness is endless. I need You to make good on that promise, because right now in my life, I need to believe in your perpetual love. I have hoped for so much, and often I've been terribly disappointed. Sometimes things just don't work out, and I feel let down. I think I'm trying to live a good life. I think I know what You expect from me, so I get frustrated when things don't go my way. God, I need to know You are near, for I cannot bear being disappointed by life and also by You.

Psalm 119 has more verses than thirteen books in the Old Testament and sixteen in the New Testament.

Distractions

Turn my eyes away from looking at worthless things.
Revive me in your ways.

Psalm 119:37, WEB

The psalmist wants to live his life in a way that pleases God and that follows God's laws. He knows that by paying too much attention to the things of this world, he will weaken or lose his connections to those things that truly matter, including his relationship with his God.

God, life is one big distraction, and I need Your help to keep my eyes on what's important. I find it hard to stay focused and to prioritize my time, my money, and my responsibilities. I spot things in flashy store windows that I want but that would gobble up my budget. Glossy magazines tout the latest clothes and hawk the newest home fashions, and lure me into daydreams about a different life. My thumbs fly along my electronic gadgets and pull me into a world of cyber conversations while I ignore the real people sitting next to me. Help me to find a way around all these tempting detours and to concentrate on You and those I love.

An acrostic poem, Psalm 119 has twenty-two stanzas; each one highlights one of the twenty-two letters in the Hebrew alphabet.

Dreams

We see not our signs:
there is no more any prophet:
neither is there among us any that knoweth how long.

Psalm 74:9, KJV

Living in exile, the Israelites feel lost. Forced from a homeland overrun with death and destruction, they find themselves in a strange land. Nowhere do they see the signs of their faith—their temple with the Ark of the Covenant. They listen for prophets who will reveal God's word, but they hear nothing. Truly, God seems to have dropped them into their enemy's clutches.

People need a little help to make their dreams come true. They need leaders with ideas and influence to make our communities better places for everyone. Sometimes I feel betrayed by those who put their greed before other's dreams. Where's the little guy's dream for a home of his own, for a good education for his kids, and healthcare, and jobs with decent wages? I look around, but I can't find leaders who want to guide us to a better future. I listen, but I don't hear inspiring plans. They're not thinking about our dreams; instead, they focus on their own ambitions. God, don't abandon us to feckless leaders. Put some ethics in their hearts even as You put some patience into ours.

The Babylonians destroyed the temple in Jerusalem in 586 BCE, which serves as an approximate date for Psalm 74.

Environment

When I consider Your heavens, the work of your fingers,
the moon and the stars, which you have ordained;
what is man, that you think of him?
What is the son of man, that you care for him?
You make him ruler over the works of Your hands.

Psalm 8:3–4, 6a, WEB

In Genesis, the Israelites learned that they were made in God's image and that God had done the unimaginable—God had handed over creation to human beings to use for their sustenance and welfare. God offered such a magnificent gift to beings placed just beneath the angels. How God loved His children!

God, we have failed to treasure this stunning orb, spinning majestically in the heavens. We have treated this planet so shabbily, and I can barely say aloud what You already know. We pollute the seas with sewage, befoul our air with chemicals, and shear the forests without concern for erosion. We dump our trash in the meadows and put ourselves in danger of destroying our very home. Guide me away from guilt and cringes of remorse and toward action. Give me courage to speak for this earth, our God-given gift. Give me wisdom as I struggle to find a more responsible way to live in the world that came to me through Your spirit of love.

Some call Psalm 8 "the astronomer's psalm," because the night sky led the psalmist to consider God's power and generosity.

Faith

Hear my prayer, O Lord, and give ear unto my cry;
hold not thy peace at my tears:
for I am a stranger with thee, and a sojourner,
as all my fathers were.

Psalm 39:12, KJV

In a Job-like moment of suffering, the psalmist pours his heart out to God. Yes, he is a sinner, but surely God will not abandon him. He considers Abraham, Isaac, and Jacob—ancestors who were aliens in new lands—and God did not abandon them nor future generations, even when they tested God. The psalmist also ponders the shortness of life; he is but a sojourner, someone who is just passing through. In his melancholy, he broods over his connection to God.

I've been well-schooled in thoughts of heaven, God. I can picture the clouds, the angels, Your heavenly throne. Heaven: It's everyone's hoped-for destination. Most days my faith gives me confidence that I'll be there. However, imagining heaven does not guarantee that Your home will one day also be mine. The psalmist knows he's just passing through this life, and I also know this life is short. Eternity, however, is forever, and I need to have faith that, just as You are with me in this moment, I will one day be with You forever.

Psalm 39 echoes the Book of Job and Ecclesiastes, two works that ponder suffering and the shortness of life.

Family

Behold, how good and how pleasant it is
For brothers to dwell together in unity!
It is like the dew of Hermon
Coming down upon the mountains of Zion;

Psalm 133:1, 3a, NASB

As their numbers grew, the Hebrews faced the challenge of feeling disconnected from those tribes that lived in distant places and whom they rarely saw. When these extended families could once again unite in Jerusalem, the wise king reminded them that living peacefully together was a blessing from God, a blessing as life-giving as the waters of snowcapped Mount Hermon.

God, I could use a little peaceful togetherness in this family. My ears ache from the squabbling, the outbursts, and the slamming doors. If the brothers and sisters of the Twelve Tribes of Israel could unite and live in harmony, why can't the children under my roof? I need Your voice telling me that these quarrelsome days shall pass. I need Your wisdom reminding me that the future holds the moment when this bickering brood will be eager to come together and will look forward to gathering at the same table to share a meal. Until that time, give me patience and give the cantankerous quieter voices.

Verse 1 is the opening line in *Life Together*, the classic book on brotherhood by theologian Dietrich Bonhoeffer.

Friends

For there is no faithfulness in their mouth.
Their heart is destruction.
Their throat is an open tomb.
They flatter with their tongue.

Psalm 5:9, WEB

Disloyal men beset the psalmist, and they may even wish him harm. What hurts is that he called those men "friends," but now he realizes they are liars. They hide evil in their hearts, and when false praise and lies come out of their mouths, the psalmist can almost smell the stench from their foul and rotten intentions. It is as though their throats are tombs filled with deceit.

God, please help me heal from the hurts inflicted by people I thought were my friends. I don't even want to think about them, because now I see them for the fakes they are. Why didn't I realize their compliments were false? Why didn't I hear their insincerities? I'm embarrassed that I was so slow to catch on and that now I'm the butt of their gossip. Maybe I was too needy to see the truth. Help me to remember that I don't need to put up with phonies, and I don't need pretend friends. Please give me a slightly thicker skin as I feel my way in this hard time.

Some think David, who had many enemies, wrote and sang Psalm 5 as a reminder that God rejects the wicked.

Happiness

My soul is weary with sorrow:
strengthen me according to your word.

Psalm 119:28, WEB

More than the desert heat caused the Hebrews to melt. Life itself dissolved their resolve and forced them to call to God for strength. They had to survive their enemies, their enslavements, and their detours from God and his word. Each time their misery abated when God answered their pleas.

Thaw out my heart, God, for in my misery I can feel it hardening against all happiness. My anger and disappointments consume me; not one positive thing has happened lately. Not one. Everything and everyone I encounter exasperates me, and my impatience with life makes me edgy with You. Help me; give me the strength You gave your desert children. Don't leave me despondent; help me to see past my gloom and into Your love, for I must not be a slave to pessimism. Let happiness, not despair, dissolve my heart into You.

Each of this psalm's twenty-two stanzas contains eight lines, and each line contains a reference to God's laws.

Health

He shall call upon me, and I will answer him:
I will be with him in trouble;
I will deliver him, and honour him.
With long life will I satisfy him,
and shew him my salvation.

Psalm 91:15–16, KJV

The Hebrews knew the dangers of life—marauders came unannounced, plagues stole entire families, and wars and famine brought suffering and death. These fears lived with them, but so did their belief in the saving power of their God.

God, I'm crying out to You. Hear me. I have fallen into troubling times, for illness has taken me prisoner, and I can feel myself falling into despair. Why me? Why now? Can I fight this? I can barely look into my loved ones' eyes, because their gaze tells me they are worried; they are praying. I want answers from doctors, even as I know You are my health authority. When all I want is You as my caregiver, nurses bring no comfort. I need to believe that You are near and that You will save me, and I need Your reassurance now. Answer me and help me to feel Your comfort.

A powerful song of trust, Psalm 91 ends not with the psalmist's voice, but the voice of God.

Home

I have gone astray like a lost sheep;
seek thy servant;
for I do not forget thy commandments.

Psalm 119:176, KJV

The psalmist calls out to God asking for help, but also proclaiming his love of God's law. God's words, he knows, will keep him on the right path, so in every line of his poem, he mentions God's instructions.

I feel lost, adrift in my life and without roots. I have an address, but I sure don't feel like I have a home, at least not with You. So God, I'm asking You to come and find me, for I feel like a homeless person who's wandered far away and can't buy a bus ticket back. I confess that it's hard to pray and sometimes it's hard to believe in You, much less myself, but I feel this urge to invite You back into my life. I suspect that the way back to You may also be the way back to myself. Whisper Your guidance into my ear and give me the guts to listen, because this lamb is lost and has gone astray. Remind me, God, that You are my foundation. Hug me close and bring me back into Your flock, because my confidence clearly has gone missing.

With its 176 verses, Psalm 119 is the longest chapter in the Hebrew Bible.

Loneliness

My God, my God, why hast thou forsaken me?
why art thou so far from helping me,
and from the words of my roaring?

Psalm 22:1, KJV

The psalmist is tormented. No prayerful whispers for him; he roars his distress to God. While he laments that God has abandoned him, he can't keep himself from calling out to his only hope for deliverance. In his suffering—physical and emotional—he believes that only God can save him, and his faith overrides his fear and desolation.

I know Jesus spoke those words while alone and suffering on the cross. How forlorn he must have felt, abandoned by everyone except a few loved ones weeping at his feet. I know nothing in my life can compare to the desertion of Jesus' friends, but I also know I'm not Jesus. I'm weak. Some days I can't face my own loneliness. I live in the world, but I feel banished from its joys, and I yearn to move from being a loner in life to a full participant. God, I know You did not abandon Jesus. Help me to remember that You have not abandoned me and that You will guide me toward a time when I will not feel so lonesome.

Because Jesus utters these words on the cross, many see Psalm 22 as a Messianic psalm foretelling Christ's passion.

Money

Yahweh, my heart isn't haughty,
nor my eyes lofty;
nor do I concern myself with great matters,
or things too wonderful for me.

Psalm 131:1, WEB

The psalmist sings of humility. Perhaps he is humble because he knows God has forgiven him for something he has done or has failed to do. So, he stands before God with a meek spirit and lowered eyes. He trusts that God knows his heart and the truth of his words.

I know money is a blessing, God, but I'm worried it will speak for me in ways that send the wrong message. Please don't let money and what it can buy change how I treat others or how I see myself. I've been fortunate and I can afford some things that others cannot, but I don't want my greater spending power to turn me into a smaller person. Help me not to sound boastful or to have a smug look on my face. I want always to treat others with respect and warmth and to remember that a thicker wallet doesn't buy me influence or status. I know You still want me to walk humbly with my God.

Preacher Charles Spurgeon said Psalm 131 was one of the shortest to read, but one of the longest to learn.

Nature

God, when you went forth before your people,
when you marched through the wilderness...Selah.
The earth trembled.
The sky also poured down rain at the presence of the God of Sinai—
at the presence of God, the God of Israel.

Psalm 68:7–8, WEB

Forty years wandering in the desert tested the Israelites, and sometimes they wavered in their faith. God, however, did not waver in devotion. When the desert proved too cruel, God stepped in to help His people, and the earth shook in obedience to its creator.

Sometimes my piece of this earth tries my patience, and my faith in the goodness of nature wavers. Downpours flood basements and wash away homes. Heat waves bake lawns and flower beds, and dry up the reservoirs. Freezing temperatures break our pipes and turn our roads into treacherous ice rinks. God, give me the patience to endure what feels like a battle between nature and humans, for I want to live in harmony with Your creation and its power and beauty. Help me to remember that, just as You made the desert relent and spare the Israelites, You stand ready to assist us when Your creation seems too daunting; we have only to ask.

Selah appears seventy-one times in the Book of Psalms. Some think it directs readers to "stop and think about it."

Neighbor

You make us an object of contention to our neighbors,
And our enemies laugh among themselves.
O God of hosts, restore us
And cause Your face to shine upon us, and we will be saved.

Psalm 80:6–7, NASB

The Hebrews were beset by enemies—perhaps their Assyrian neighbors or the marauding Babylonians. In their fear and grief, they lift a communal lament to God. Why, they ask, would God free us from Egyptian bondage, protect us in the desert, and build us into a great nation only to let neighbors destroy us? Surely, God has not abandoned us. May he look on us again with his favor and love.

You gave us a command, "Thou shalt love thy neighbor as thyself" (Mk 12:31, KJV); but it was easier to follow Your instruction when my neighbors looked like me. I care about the people I see at my grocery store; we stroll on the same sidewalks. However, the world now reaches beyond my neighborhood. Twitter, Facebook, and twenty-four hour news channels pull me into foreign neighborhoods where people speak unfamiliar languages and wear clothing I can't find in my closet. Are these people my neighbors? Must I love them when I don't understand them? I know Your answer; what I don't know is how to live it.

The Babylonian invasion of 586 BCE destroyed or defamed everything the Israelites held sacred.

Networking

But as for me, I will walk in my integrity.
Redeem me, and be merciful to me.

Psalm 26:11, WEB

The psalmist promises God that he will be upright in the future. Maybe he hasn't always been honorable. Perhaps others have accused him of misdeeds. It doesn't matter, for regardless of his sins, God will forgive and be merciful. From this day forward, he walks with God.

I can't blame my electronics. These boxes of plastic and wires with touch screens and apps did not send the words; I did. My Facebook page did not post the comments and unflattering pictures; I did. At the time, it all seemed harmless, maybe even funny, but then people got hurt and retorts from cyberspace landed on my screen. I could hear the anger in their comebacks, and I cringed. What was I thinking? I'm not some emotionally charged teenager who goes off on others just because he can. I'm not someone who spouts off with the first thing that comes into her head. God, I'm embarrassed, and it's hard to face my thoughtless words. Please help me from this day forward to behave with integrity and to be a good cybercitizen who treats others well.

The Psalter is divided into five books to correspond with the Torah, the first five books of the Bible.

Noise

Give ear to my prayer, O God;
and hide not thyself from my supplication.
Attend unto me, and hear me;
I mourn in my complaint, and make a noise.

Psalm 55:1–2, KJV

The Israelites' moanings and groanings thundered heavenward, but God did not ignore their irksome petitions. With patience, he listened to their woes and came to their aid. When they complained of hunger and thirst, God sent manna and delivered water from stones. They knew they could trust God to hear them.

When life doesn't go my way, I complain. When I feel rushed and distracted, I am known to sigh in exasperation. Too much work makes me moan, and heavy burdens find me groaning with annoyance. At these times, I'm not easy to be around. Either I proclaim my troubles noisily, giving voice to my inner agitations, or I stew in silence loudly enough to hush those who must tiptoe around me. I admit it—I'm noisy when I'm unhappy. Help me to remember to turn to You when I am hurting and want to rant, for Your ears can endure my strident tones, and Your unwavering love will quiet my vexations and turn my protests into calm.

Some believe that verses 1–2 are King David's voice calling out to God following the betrayal of David's son Absalom.

People

Vindicate me, Lord,
for I have led a blameless life;
I have trusted in the Lord
and have not faltered.

Psalm 26:1, NIV

Confident that he has led a good life, the psalmist stands before his God and declares his innocence. He is unwavering in his trust that God will pronounce him not guilty and he will hold his head high among his accusers.

I'm not what gossiping people say I am, yet it's so hard to ignore the hurtful words I've overheard. Does a person's raised eyebrows mean he questions my integrity and believes the rumors? When someone quickly turns away to avoid my gaze, does that mean she thinks I've done something wrong? I want to shout, "I've done nothing. Don't believe the gossips. Haven't you always known me to be truthful?" Nevertheless, I fear people will ignore my words and instead be swayed by untruths. You know the truth, God. I'm not perfect, but I am not what people say. I can calm my fears of a damaged reputation if You help me to remember that You know the truth; You know I have tried my very best.

Because it professes a blameless heart, Psalm 26 was among those the Israelites sang before offering a sacrifice.

Popularity

You love evil more than good,
lying rather than speaking the truth. Selah.
You love all devouring words,
you deceitful tongue.

Psalm 52:3–4, WEB

The psalmist knows the story of David when he hid from King Saul and accepted bread and a sword from Achimelech, a priest in Nob. Doeg, who served Saul, saw Achimelech help David and reported him to Saul. Then on Saul's command, he slew not only Achimelech, but also all the priests of Nob and their families. The poet reminds the listeners that Doeg's desire to curry Saul's favor caused the deaths of countless innocents.

God, help me to stand up for others. As a kid, I watched classmates get bullied while others—including me—stood silent, averting our eyes, hoping the bully would not direct threats our way or doom us to unpopularity. Today, I often feel spineless against gossips. When I hear someone spreading hearsay about another, I often pretend I haven't heard the snide remarks. Give me the courage to stand up for others and to say, "Stop, he's my friend," even if my comments mean I lose someone's approval.

The story of David, Achimelech, the chief herdsman Doeg, and King Saul can be found in I Samuel, Chapters 21–22.

But I am poor and needy.
May the Lord think about me.
You are my help and my deliverer.
Don't delay, my God.

Psalm 40:17, WEB

Earlier the psalmist extolled God for his generosity and protection, but then he remembers a troubling piece. While it's true that God has been kind, the psalmist admits that he's still needy, maybe even miserable. In his poverty he cries out, "God, don't forget this small, lowly creature calling to You for help."

God, I say "I want more" instead of "I have plenty." I've been known to whine, "I've just got to buy that," instead of "There's nothing else I need," and I'm guilty of turning to retail therapy when I'm blue or bored. Even as I spend money, I fret about paying the bills and saving enough for retirement. Though I'm surrounded by stuff, I admit it: I still want more. In spite of those moments when the shopping malls lure me and television ads beckon, I know in my heart that You have given me everything and anything I could possibly want. I do not know poverty, so help me to say "I have enough. I'm content."

➢ **The sentiments of Verse 17 resonated with the psalmist, for they also can be found in Psalms 35 and 70.**

Relationships

I am weary with my groaning.
Every night I flood my bed.
I drench my couch with my tears.

Psalm 6:6, WEB

In the psalmist's time, people wailed loudly, audibly expressing overpowering emotions. Perhaps grief has conquered the psalmist or physical pain tortures him. Possibly, he simply needs to expose a deeply human moment of self-pity. Whatever his trials, he sorrowfully calls out to God.

I'm not like the psalmist, God, yowling from my bedroom so everyone can hear me. My tears embarrass me. When relationship struggles find me crying myself to sleep, I muffle my sadness with pillows and covers. I don't want others to know that a broken heart sends me sobbing under my quilt. I want to be strong enough to let critical remarks from a co-worker roll off me rather than have tears stream down my cheeks. I don't want my friends to know that snubs make me snivel. God, I don't want to be so emotionally fragile that relationship struggles send me into emotional tailspins. Knowing I can't hide my quiet sorrows from You helps lift me out of the doldrums. Please, I need Your help to grow stronger or less shy about letting others know I'm sad.

Seven psalms are Penitential Psalms—the great laments—and Psalm 6 is the first of these in the Psalter.

Retirement

Who is the man who delights in life,
loving a long life to enjoy what is good?

Psalm 34:12, HCSB

The psalmist asks, "Who wants to live a long life?" The answer seems obvious—everyone, especially if that life can include health and happiness. Yet the psalmist asks who is willing to weave mercy and blessings into those later years so that long life and righteousness blend together?

I can't wait for retirement. I want to wake up each morning knowing that I'm the one who gets to decide how to spend my time. God, as much as I long for this freedom from a daily job, I know I'll need Your help to spend my free time wisely. Bless me with a long retirement, but also help me to be a blessing to others. What's the point of living through several decades, if I can't see that the world was made better because I spent time here? Teach me now how to be useful and how to fill my retirement years with good works. Because when I'm too frail to continue, I want to be able to sit back knowing I did some good.

Psalm 34 inspired the popular hymn "Taste and See."

Safety

In my distress I called upon the Lord,
and cried unto my God:
he heard my voice out of his temple,
and my cry came before him, even into his ears.

Psalm 18:6, KJV

The poet, possibly David, vividly recalls a difficult moment when he feared for his life and called to God. The Israelites knew by heart the details of King David's life, so the poet's retelling in this psalm does more than simply refresh their memories. It also helps them relive the spiritual triumph of their king. The psalmist also reminds them that in times of trouble, they can imitate their king and call out to God, who will hear them.

I wish my faith were stronger so that in all of life's moments I would know that I am safe, because You are with me. It's easy to feel secure when life goes well. Few scaredy cats tremble and look over their shoulders when the sun is out and friends surround them. Yet on those days when the roads seem too slippery, or when thunderclouds darken the skies, or the news announces a rash of home break-ins, I find myself double-checking my door locks and deciding to stay indoors. Strengthen my faith so that I can feel secure in You.

David's prominence as a poet is indicated in 2 Samuel 23:1, where he is called "the sweet psalmist of Israel."

Self-confidence

May Yahweh answer you in the day of trouble.
May the name of the God of Jacob set you up on high,
send you help from the sanctuary, grant you support from Zion,
We will triumph in your salvation.

Psalm 20:1–2, 5a, WEB

The psalmist directly addresses the king and his armies as they head out to face the enemy. The faithful who stay behind in the temple recall their patriarch Jacob and the success of his twelve tribes. Taking comfort from what God promised to Jacob, they join their voices in a song of hope for success in battle and a safe return.

I don't feel up to tackling the tasks before me or making any decisions to change things in my life. I hear others talk about designing a big project at work or plans to change jobs, and I'm cowed by their perseverance and self-assurance. I'm not even brave enough to voice my concerns or dreams to others, because change and challenge overwhelm me. I know my fears defeat me before I even begin and erode any confidence I might have for success. God, give me a healthy dose of optimism and stand close to me as I take on the big and little battles in my life. Help me to believe that I'll triumph.

Zion refers to both the capital of Jerusalem and God's sanctuary in the holiest of temples.

Setbacks

In the daytime also he led them with a cloud,
and all the night with a light of fire.
He clave the rocks in the wilderness,
and gave them drink as out of the great depths.

Psalm 78:14–15, KJV

As the psalmist reveals, God stepped in often to aid the Israelites. He provided signs to direct them through the desert and offered water at crucial times; and yet, the Israelites were not always grateful. They saw their time in the desert as one of torment and a deceptive promise about a new land. God, however, saw their desert sojourn as a time of testing and recommitment.

God, this feels like a desert moment in my life. I'm lost and going nowhere. Some days, I feel as if I've lost ground with my career and with my blueprint for a successful life. It feels like I've been overcome by inertia forever. I want fewer setbacks and more triumphs. You helped the Hebrews. They were lost, thirsty, and afraid, and You moved them forward again, even as You wanted them to recommit themselves to You. I trust that You're willing to help me, but are these setbacks my test? Are You asking me to reflect on You and my goals during this barren time in my life?

A hymn based on Psalm 78 has been sung at Harvard University's commencement since 1806.

Sexuality

Have mercy upon me, O God,
according to thy loving-kindness:
according unto the multitude of thy tender mercies
blot out my transgressions.

Psalm 51:1, KJV

The speaker, who has blatantly sinned, begs God for forgiveness and to be made whole. In earlier lines, the psalmist suggests that the sinner is David, who lusted for Bathsheba, committed adultery, and then arranged for her husband's murder—blatant sins, indeed. In spite of his grave offenses, the sinner hopes God will show mercy, put his sins aside, and let him start his spiritual life anew.

I want to cry out, "God, have mercy on me and blot out my sins!" I want to start fresh. I want to recapture some of the innocence I felt when I was younger and my body felt exciting and I dreamed about romantic moments and "happily ever after." I'm not sure where I went wrong. I thought that my flirtations were part of being free and that sex for the excitement would turn into love somewhere along the way. However, it didn't, and I turn to You to help me ease this disappointment in myself and to set me on a new path.

Psalm 51, often referred to as *Miserere*, begins with the words *Miserere mei, Deus*—"Have mercy on me God."

Sleep

I laid me down and slept;
I awaked; for the Lord sustained me.
I will not be afraid of ten thousands of people,
that have set themselves against me round about.

Psalm 3:5–6, KJV

In his lament, the psalmist is beset by enemies, whether in dreams facing thousands of opponents or in the fields where real adversaries lurk outside his tent. In spite of these foes, he can lie down and fall asleep, because he puts his trust in God to sustain him.

My dreams tell me I am beset by opponents. I don't recognize them from my day life, but at night, clearly they find me and raid my slumber. I once thought only children suffered from nightmares, but these frights are steady visitors in my grown-up world. It's hard to fall asleep knowing that likely I'll wake fearful and whimpering. People tell me I must be worried about something; perhaps I'm fighting off a virus, they suggest. I can't identify the enemy within or without that haunts my sleep, so I turn to You to help me do battle with my dreams. God, it's hard to fight the night alone; I need the protection of Your shield to help me put my worries to rest and welcome sleep.

Psalm 3 is the first of the many Psalter laments or appeals to God to intervene and make something better.

Solitude

But I am poor and needy.
Come to me quickly, God.
You are my help and my deliverer.
Yahweh, don't delay.

Psalm 70:5, WEB

The psalmist addresses God with urgency. Clearly, he needs immediate help, for he stresses that God should come quickly and aid him now. Is he facing an enemy? Has illness overshadowed him or a loved one? Has he fallen into a dark hole of sadness? The reason for haste pales in comparison to his belief that God will answer and help him.

I like being alone, and usually I have no trouble telling the difference between alone time and lonely time. One often includes soft music and peaceful thoughts, and the other leaves me feeling pitiful. These days, however, I think I might be contracting a case of the blues. My friends say, "We hardly see you," and I'm thinking, "I just need to be alone." So, I'm not sure if I'm craving solitude or simply withdrawing from the world. I want balance in my life—a little quiet and a little activity—but I'm struggling to figure myself out. Am I seeking solitude or am I wallowing in self-pity? Help me figure this puzzle out.

Psalms of lament, which include Psalm 70, are clustered within the first three books of the Psalter.

Strangers

Don't hold the iniquities of our forefathers against us.
Let your tender mercies speedily meet us,
for we are in desperate need.

Psalm 79:8, WEB

The psalm is a lament on the destruction of the temple in Jerusalem. Whether the massacre and devastation are fresh in the psalmist's memory or live in his imagination through the stories of his ancestors, he feels an acute sense of loss. Did God punish the Hebrews so severely because of sins committed by their forbears? God, he calls out, don't hold a grudge, but look on those of us in need.

I am ashamed that too often people have been inhospitable to Your children. Instead of reaching out to the marginalized, such as migrant workers, the mentally ill, those suffering with AIDS, or refugees seeking asylum, we have treated them shamefully. Instead of our love, they faced our prisons, billy clubs, hate signs, and neglect. Sometimes we struggle with the Golden Rule; often we fear those who are different or those we deem unworthy. We have failed You and our brothers and sisters so many times in the past. Do not hold our failings against us. Please let us start afresh, God, in opening our hearts to the outcasts among us.

Some biblical historians think Psalm 79 specifically refers to the Babylonian conquest in 586 BCE.

Strength

Let your hand be on the man of your right hand,
on the son of man whom you made strong for yourself.
So we will not turn away from you.
Revive us, and we will call on your name.

Psalm 80:17–18, WEB

God, the psalmist laments, you made us strong, so that we could survive in an unforgiving land. You nurtured us and depended on us to build your kingdom, so why turn away? Our enemies attack us, but we still believe you will defend us. We have only to call your name, and you will stand with us.

I believe that I should stand up for the weak and help those who suffer, but I'm finding that it's tough to do the work of Your kingdom. Why are conversations about immigration, or racial profiling, or a fair wage more about accusations and less about solving problems? When did it become unpatriotic to believe that Muslims, Jews, and Christians are all Your children? I want to champion good causes, but my strength fades when I think about the angry faces and accusing tones that I'll encounter. I find it hard to take a stand, God, so stand close to me. I need to feel Your strength so my resolve holds steady.

It is likely that Assyrian aggression against the Northern Kingdom of Israel, around 720 BCE, inspired this psalm.

Terrorism

Praise the Lord, all nations!
Glorify Him, all peoples!
For His faithful love to us is great;
the Lord's faithfulness endures forever.
Hallelujah!

Psalm 117:1–2, HCSB

The psalmist summons all nations, not just Israel, to praise God. He calls all peoples, not just the Hebrews, to glorify the Lord. In exchange for unanimity, God would be forever faithful to all. If the psalmist had called a world summit in the Land of Canaan, this would be the gathering's sacred song.

God, surely You shake Your head at Jews, Muslims, and Christians—all children of Father Abraham and You—who embroil themselves in acts of terrorism. Those who make bombs, those who carry weapons of terror into public places, those who support terrorism and those who fight against it, and those maimed and the dead innocents are all in need of Your care. Thousands of years ago, in a land torn by religious strife, the psalmist envisioned an accord among all peoples. Please send a new song of peace and fresh ears to hear it, so that all might unite in praise of You.

With only two verses, Psalm 117 is the shortest psalm.

Theft

The wicked borrow, and don't pay back,
but the righteous give generously.

Psalm 37:21, WEB

Like people everywhere, the Hebrews sometimes complained that life wasn't fair. Others took advantage of them, but the evildoers never were punished. Sometimes the unrighteous faired better than the God-fearing. The Hebrews grumbled, "Why are they happy and successful though they ignore God, while the faithful struggle?" Take the long view, the psalm urges, for in time, life balances out.

I feel taken advantage of, so that some days it seems everyone is a potential pickpocket, taking from me what I don't want to give or lose. I'm annoyed with folks who steal my time with gossip and idle chatter, and if that chatter turns to worrisome things, then they've pinched my peace of mind as well. The thoughtless or the unkind pilfer my confidence in others, and the whiny pessimists rob me of my hopeful outlook. Like the wicked in the psalmist's poem, some people take and never give back. God, it's hard to deal with this thievery of the heart and spirit. Help me to hold on to my hopes and shore up a generous spirit within me, so that I don't feel burdened by these robbers.

A wisdom psalm, Psalm 37 reassures the faithful that the wicked eventually will fair poorly in this life.

Time

So teach us to number our days,
that we may gain a heart of wisdom.

Psalm 90:12, WEB

The Israelites knew of long-lived relatives who saw life spans that exceeded centuries; but even a Methuselah living beyond 900 years lived but a second compared to the eternity of God. Thousands of years ago, the Israelites understood what we understand, but do not like: life is fleeting.

Life feels like a race, and most days I don't make it to the finish line of my To Do list. I dash to work and race to appointments. I speed-text and fast-talk; the faces of loved ones rush by and I haven't even noticed if they were smiling. Life, a life worth living and remembering, has to hold more than seconds zipped through and forgotten. God, this is the only life I have, so please teach me how to value my days and spend my seconds like the treasure that they are. I can't count my remaining days on Earth—that is a secret You hold—but with Your help, I can wisely spend my gift of time so that moments with others and with You are rich in love.

Isaac Watts' hymn, "O God, Our Help in Ages Past," puts Psalm 90 to music.

Violence

Deliver me, O my God, out of the hand of the wicked, out of the hand of the unrighteous and cruel man.

Psalm 71:4, KJV

The Israelites had many enemies. Their foes sought to slaughter them, take their herds, enslave their women and children, and sack their temple. They fought ferocious desert battles and each time called to God for rescue and victory.

God, in the desert of my life, I read about home invasions and car jackings. Headlines scream the news of murders, kidnappings, rapes, and robberies. I do not want to have a gun thrust in my face, to have children I know snatched into strange cars. I'm afraid of those who will hurt me. I lock and double-lock my doors. I look over my shoulder when I walk outside and startle at strange sounds that amount to nothing. I want to let go of this fear, because it keeps me from living fully. Rescue me not only from those who might harm me, but also from my own terrors, which haunt my imagination and hold me captive. Help me to remember that, like the Israelites, I can call on You because You stand near me ready to give me the strength to step into life without trembles.

Reformer Dorothy Day said, "My strength returns to me with my cup of coffee and the reading of the psalms."

War

Nor for the pestilence that walketh in darkness;
nor for the destruction that wasteth at noonday.
A thousand shall fall at thy side,
and ten thousand at thy right hand;
but it shall not come nigh thee.

Psalm 91:6–7, KJV

When thousands drop from deadly diseases and when war captures others' lives, the psalmist reminds the Hebrews that they will stay strong. No swords shall pierce them and turn them into corpses. God will protect them, because they believe.

God, men and women are in harm's way serving this country. A few I know and ache for, but all are deserving of Your care. I need to believe that those I love and those carried tenderly in others' hearts will be spared. Soldiers in fatigues battle through heat, dust, fear, and exhaustion on my television screen. I don't know their names, but I know You do, and You know the names of those I lift to You in prayer each day. I want to be like the psalmist and believe that in deserts and mountains loved ones will not be harmed; their deaths or injuries will not break the hearts of all who love them.

A book of psalms was the first book published in the colonies: *The Bay Psalm Book* in 1640, in Massachusetts.

Work

Let the favor of the Lord our God be on us;
establish the work of our hands for us;
yes, establish the work of our hands.

Psalm 90:17, WEB

For forty years, Moses led a wandering people through the desert. He toiled and struggled with an unruly people. In faith he lived, but he died before he crossed the Jordan River into the Promised Land, though he could see it in the distance. Others reaped the rewards of his labors, but he did not live to see their joy.

I work hard, Lord, and I want my work to count for something more than just a paycheck. I want to know that my struggles today will benefit others tomorrow, whether those are my family, my colleagues, my neighbors, or my fellow worshippers. Don't let me leave this world without having made a difference, without having left a mark. God, smile on my efforts and make my life matter. Let your favor rest on the work of my hands, and my heart, and my mind, so that what I strive to do matters in Your great plan. Help me to remember that Moses did not know what history teaches me—he mattered to the generations to come, and with Your help, so shall I.

Some scholars think Psalm 90 is the oldest of the psalms, perhaps written after the Israelites' flight from Egypt.

Worry

My heart is sore pained within me:
and the terrors of death are fallen upon me.
Fearfulness and trembling are come upon me,
and horror hath overwhelmed me.

Psalm 55:4–5, KJV

Fear ensnares the psalmist. He sings of those who malign his good name and of friends who have turned from him in hate. Enemies lurk everywhere. Yet, he speaks of no actual harm that has happened, only the worry that life no longer feels secure. In his terrors, he finds he can turn to no one but God.

I can't seem to shake the fears that grip me and the questions that twirl in my head. What will tomorrow bring? Do they love me? Am I good enough? Will she like my present? Will he think I'm good looking? I know these questions are foolish, God, still they spin in my head and sap my spirit. You ask me to put my faith in You and to trust that no matter the outcome, my life stands secure if it stands within You. I hear those words, God; now help me to believe them. I want hope, not hand wringing. I need Your hand to rest gently on my shoulder and settle my anxious heart.

Felix Mendelssohn's work "Hear My Prayer" set the text of Psalm 55 to music.

Praise

God, You are the best

Aging

Who satisfies your desire with good things,
so that your youth is renewed like the eagle's.

Psalm 103:5, WEB

God gave his Hebrew children all that they needed. The prophet Isaiah told them that if they placed their hope in the Lord and followed his way, they would soar with strength and never grow weary.

God, I'm growing older, but I'm not buying wrinkle cream, because I'm growing young in You. You were wise when You urged me to grow my love and need for You, for even as I become more dependent on You, I feel stronger. Isn't that funny: Strength coming from leaning? Renewal coming from reliance? You promised Your children eternal life, if only we believed. Now as my life shortens in years and my body tires more easily, I feel more robust and more resilient, not only in faith, but also in my life. I'm not a kid anymore, but I feel the optimism and energy that I once thought was reserved only for the young. You are my Fountain of Youth. God, help me always to feel as spiritually strong and healthy as I do right now, and to smile at words like "old," because I know that through You I am stronger than ever.

Flying high and with great strength, the eagle symbolizes youth and vigor for the poet of Psalm 103.

Death

The cords of death surrounded me,
the pains of Sheol got a hold of me.
I found trouble and sorrow.
Then called I upon the name of Yahweh:
Yahweh, I beg you, deliver my soul.

Psalm 116:3–4, WEB

Seriously ill and dreading his impending grave, the psalmist cried out to God, "Lord, save me!" Though ensnared by fear and sorrow, he remembered that even in the hardest of times, he could turn to God, and God answered and spared his life. Soon he could proclaim, "The Lord saved me," and from that pronouncement flowed his praise.

Like the psalmist, God, I truly believed I was dying. Family gazed at me tearfully, friends whispered their good wishes, nurses stepped lightly around my bed, and my once strong body grew weaker. The pain did not abate. Those moments, however, are simply memories, for I survived, and I stepped back into my life a much wiser person. Having faced death, I now realize how precious is Your gift of my life. You restored more than my health, God. You bestowed on me the gift of gratefulness, and each day I revel in the sweetness of life.

For Israelites, Sheol was a place of quiet darkness where all souls—the just and the unjust—went after death.

Decisions

Your word is a lamp to my feet
And a light to my path.

Psalm 119:105, NASB

The Israelites knew what it was to walk in the ink-black night; only a fool would venture out without a lantern to brighten the path directly in front of his sandals. How else could someone keep from tumbling into trash, tripping over rocks, or facing unseen dangers?

You are my lantern, God. Some days I feel like I'm groping in darkness. What's the right decision? What's the right action? I don't want to stumble and fall; I don't want to make the wrong choices. I want to go for what's best for my life. Thank goodness, I can walk confidently, because You light my way. How many times have I heard Your guiding voice in my ear? How many times have You sent me directions through inspiring hymns and pulpit proclamations? Your word is the beam that lights up the route of my life. Help me always to remember that even when the pathway seems dim, I only have to flip Your switch to find my way again.

As a prayer, Psalm 119 urges the faithful to reflect on God's laws.

Depression

For he remembered his holy word,
and Abraham, his servant.
He brought forth his people with joy,
his chosen with singing.

Psalm 105:42–43, WEB

The psalmist gladly recounts the Israelites' history of struggles and deliverance. God promised Abraham that he would make him the father of a great nation, and in turn, Abraham and his descendants promised to be faithful to God. The psalmist sings tribute to God for saving his people from their sorrows when the Israelites wandered homeless and hungry in the desert.

God, I was lost in the desert of my own life. So tired and empty inside, I longed for deliverance, but I could find neither help nor escape. I think You must have tapped me on the shoulder, because one day I remembered You, and in small ways I began to give up my sadness. I prayed a little more; I cried a little less. I read Your words a bit more and slowly let go of my unhappiness. Instead of feeling encased in hopelessness, I felt Your comforting presence. Because You chose me as Your child, You remembered our covenant and delivered me. Alleluia!

➾ **Psalm 105 is considered a historical psalm because its forty-five verses recount the struggles and salvation of the Hebrews.**

Disappointment

The Lord bless you from Zion,
And may you see the prosperity of Jerusalem all the days of your life.
Indeed, may you see your children's children.
Peace be upon Israel!

Psalm 128:5–6, NASB

For the Hebrews, life's blessings and God's favor found visible proof in family—a hardworking husband, a fruitful wife, and healthy children brought daily joy. Children also meant that even after death, parents would live on through their children's children.

Blessings and disappointments—You have given both to me, God, and sometimes in the same person! You're tricky. You know that our kids, our parents, and our spouses can push our Disappointment Button harder than anyone can. I love these people fiercely, and in Your wisdom, You planned for that. You knew that a heart stuffed with love has less room for gnawing disappointment. Sure, I'm not happy with everyone all the time, or they with me, for that matter, but part of handling family frustrations also depends on me. If I put the effort into loving my family, then those moments of disappointment pale in comparison to the happiness and pride that returns to me in blessings. Each day You teach me how to work through disappointment by tempering it with love.

Psalm 128, sometimes called the "Wedding Psalm," has been set to music and sung at many nuptials.

Distractions

And I said, Oh that I had wings like a dove!
for then would I fly away, and be at rest.
Lo, then would I wander far off,
and remain in the wilderness. Selah.

Psalm 55:6–7, KJV

When troubles crowd the psalmist—enemies, fickle friends, corruption, and gossip—he takes flight into a daydream of just leaving it all behind. Like a dove, he wants to lift his white wings toward the sun and fly off to a trouble-free land. He also knows he can find respite and relief in God.

I hear frequently words like "get focused," "stay on task," "keep your eyes on the prize," and I get it. Sometimes I have to pay attention if I want to get anything done. Nevertheless, the imagination You have given me, God, is good for more than just reading a blockbuster novel or daydreaming about heaven. My amazing mind can zero in on an abundance of life-enhancing distractions—good food, a funny movie, even the newest computer game—that give me respite from the grind and help me relax. Even You, God, have been known to distract me when I stop to ponder the beauty of Your sunrises or to reflect on how well You care for me.

In Jeremiah 9, the prophet describes identical get-away feelings, suggesting to some that he also authored Psalm 55.

Dreams

You evildoers frustrate the plans of the poor,
but the Lord is their refuge.

Psalm 14:6, NIV

Like everyone else, the Israelites experienced bullies and fools. The psalmist writes from a time embroiled in corruption and godlessness, but he knows that evildoers can't fool God or people of good heart. God sees through the wicked, and virtuous people have confidence that God stands with the believers and lovers of God's laws.

I don't have much, but I have my dreams, and they carry me into each new day. Others can make fun of me, if they wish. They can laugh at me for living in my supposed fantasy world and ridicule me for believing that wonderful or exciting things will come my way. I stand by my dreams, because they grow out of gifts You have given me—my talents and my determination. I trust that You not only stand by me, but also by my dreams, for they are my heart's desires. How great You are to plant within Your children's hearts the possibilities of what they can become and what they can do. My dreams will come true and will glorify You.

Meaning "Song of Praise," *Tehillim* is the Hebrew word for the Book of Psalms.

Environment

Princes shall come out of Egypt;
Ethiopia shall soon stretch out her hands unto God.
Sing unto God, ye kingdoms of the earth;
O sing praises unto the Lord; Selah.

Psalm 68:31–32, KJV

The psalmist calls upon the powerful kingdoms of Egypt and Ethiopia to praise God and to recognize God's temple in Jerusalem and his throne on Mount Zion—the mountaintop God chose for his seat. Listen to his thundering roar as he rides across the heavens. He is ruler of all.

You have placed us in an amazing world, and the kingdoms within it recognize Your sovereignty. The kingdoms of animals and plants, the worlds inhabited by single-cell life in the boiling waters of Yellowstone or in the human body, mushrooms, and algae—these kingdoms belong to You, their creator. You have ordered their existence, and they preserve a balance with You and with each other. When I ponder our natural world, I see the wisdom and protections of a loving God. Others may be troubled by the environment's ability to survive pollution and human intrusion, but I trust the sovereign of the kingdoms to protect His creation.

The Hebrews sang this triumphal hymn when they carried the Ark of the Covenant into the temple.

Faith

I have taken refuge in the Lord.
How can you say to me,
"Escape to the mountain like a bird!"
For the Lord is righteous; He loves righteous deeds.
The upright will see His face.

Psalm 11:1, 7, HCSB

The psalmist displays a bravery built on faith. His friends tell him to flee, for the enemy is coming and will surely do him harm. The psalmist, however, never considers running away. A righteous man, he holds to his beliefs that God stands with him and against the wicked. He draws confidence from his faith and from God.

My world is not as dangerous as the poet's is; evildoers do not pursue me and I do not fear for my life. Nevertheless, I would be foolish to think that evil doesn't exist, and I would be a coward to back away from wickedness. I believe that You call me to stand my ground for what is right and that if I draw strength from my faith, then You will stand with me. My faith tells me that You want to see Your children live with honor, and like any good parent, You will reward Your children for doing what is right and for faithfully following Your decrees.

This song of trust, entitled "Unshaken Confidence in God," may recount David's feelings when Saul turned against him.

Family

He will cover you with his feathers.
Under his wings you will take refuge.
His faithfulness is your shield and rampart.

Psalm 91:4, WEB

The Israelites saw mother birds spread their wings over their nests to protect their chicks. They believed that like a mother bird, Yahweh also shielded them and gave them refuge, and they praised God for this tender care.

The people in my family are the most precious things I have, God, and I spend parts of every day thinking about their happiness and safety. I know my friends have the same focus. Did my child make it safely to school and will her friends be kind? Are mom and dad secure in their home and is the neighbor checking on them? Will my spouse have a great day at work? Were it not for You, the uncertainties could drive us all crazy, but You are with them. I know deep in my heart that my loved ones are in Your care. You have spread Your wings over my nest, and Your loving shield protects my heart and spirit.

People have lovingly prayed the psalms for thousands of years, because they capture the range of human experience and emotion.

Friends

For you make him most blessed forever.
You make him glad with joy in your presence.

Psalm 21:6, WEB

The victorious king has returned from war, and the psalmist sings in thanksgiving. For the Israelites, every threat and occurrence of war made them fear their future. No wonder it is that with joyful hearts they praise God—their deliverer and the constant presence of comfort and security in their lives.

God, how wise you were to give us friends—our eternal blessings and our source of comfort. Friends aren't as close as family, but they are the ones we've chosen to be like family. They put their feet under our dinner tables, dance at our family weddings, and watch us blow out our birthday candles—year after year. Out of all the people who pass through our lives, we've tapped these special ones to hear our secrets, accept our insecurities, and cheer us on. Sometimes when I'm sharing a moment of tears or laughter with a dear friend, I find myself silently asking, "What would I do without you?" I know the answer: I'd be lost. You knew that at those times when I might forget to turn to You, I could turn to my friends and feel Your support in their embrace.

Psalm 21, a song of victory, is paired with Psalm 20, which is a prayer before battle.

Happiness

Then will I go unto the altar of God,
unto God my exceeding joy:
yea, upon the harp will I praise thee,
O God my God.

Psalm 43:4, KJV

When the Hebrews wanted to be close to God, they went to the temple altar, the holy place where they could offer up their gifts of music and praise. There they could loudly proclaim that the God they sang to belonged to them alone.

I seek You, God, as I would a close friend, as someone I can talk to about anything. You never let Your power stand between us. You know me, and You share my happiness. Often You are the source of my happiness. The altar at church reminds me of You, but our chats have never needed a formal place. You and I can visit on the sofa, during an evening stroll, and even in the car. I'm not King David—I can't praise You with my amazing harp skills. So, let my laughter be the music that sends praises Your way. For You are my God, and I claim You as my very own.

Scholars think Psalm 43 originally ended Psalm 42. When read as one, the psalms clearly echo each other.

Health

Why, my soul, are you downcast?
Why so disturbed within me?
Put your hope in God,
for I will yet praise him,
my Savior and my God.

Psalm 42:5, NIV

The psalmist's restless inner spirit cannot be soothed, and he struggles with his agitated feelings. Is he ill or do enemies worry him? Though sad and troubled, he knows the way to a calm heart—trust in God's help. With that trust, he can fully proclaim that a faithful God is worthy of praise.

My health isn't good, and some days the merry-go-round of doctors, hospitals, and medication makes me melancholy. Nevertheless, even as my body might be ailing, I sing Your praises, because You have shown my spirit the true route to recovery. You have nurtured hope in my heart, and it glows within me like a small but steady flame. My body might be sickly, but You have given me a strong spirit that swells with trust and faith in You. Each day, You nurture my resolve to journey toward wholeness of body and soul and to keep faith with my God.

In Hebrew, the Book of Psalms is *Tehillim*, or "Song of Praise."

Home

The bird also has found a house,
And the swallow a nest for herself,
where she may lay her young,
Even Your altars, O Lord of hosts,
My King and my God.

Psalm 84:3, NASB

The psalmist has journeyed to Jerusalem to experience God's divine presence. Observing the temple grounds, he can see the sparrows and swallows that had built their nests under the eaves or onto the walls. These small beings flitted about the sanctuary, and the psalmist longed to be as close to God as the fledglings near the altar.

God, wherever I am, there You are. No matter where I live or how many times I forward my mail, You are my lifelong address. I know that, like the sparrow, I am not so small or so insignificant that You will refuse to shelter me under Your wings. Help me to remember that in Your goodness You have given me a home to live in and a home of the heart—places where I can feel secure both in a neighborhood and within Your Spirit.

The psalmist likely knew the custom among some people not to disturb nests built on or near the temples.

Loneliness

The Lord redeemeth the soul of his servants:
and none of them that trust in him shall be desolate.

Psalm 34:22, KJV

The psalmist starts his hymn with a remembrance of when King Saul tried to kill David. To save himself while in hiding, David faked insanity, because people of that time thought it wrong to kill anyone who was mentally ill. The poet reminds the prayerful that David didn't have to trick his enemies; he had only to trust in God, who would not abandon him to his foes.

Sometimes I have been my own worst enemy, isolating myself from others because I did not trust them to accept me. What if they thought my ideas crazy, my opinions weird, or my quirkiness too bizarre? Instead of braving a possible snub, I pulled inward, and like a turtle tucked tightly into its shell, I enclosed myself in protective loneliness. I remembered that I only had to stick my neck out to God, and You answered my prayers for confidence. You gave me a generous portion of trust not only in myself, but also in others. With You as my companion, I cautiously but steadily stepped out of my loneliness and back into life with others.

Because each of its verses begins with a different letter of the Hebrew alphabet, Psalm 34 is an acrostic psalm.

Money

All day long he deals graciously, and lends.
His seed is blessed.
The righteous shall inherit the land,
and live in it forever.

Psalm 37:26, 29, WEB

The psalmist reminds the Israelites that their God wants them to be a righteous and generous people who honor God's ways and care for each other. The poet draws from Deuteronomy to remind his listeners of God's promise. Those who shun evil and live honestly will prosper, "that thou mayest dwell in the land that the Lord swore unto thy fathers…" (Dt 30:20, KJV).

Where would any of us be if people hadn't lent us money? Homeowners would be in apartments, and many who drive cars would be walking or taking the bus. Who hasn't asked mom or dad to "borrow" money for gas? I'm grateful for my home, my car, and my parents' "loans," but I'm also appreciative when people have loaned me more than their dollars. I have received their time, their ideas, and their kind regard, and I hope I have repaid those debts, and then some. Above all, God, You have been the most bighearted of bankers, bestowing generously and asking only for the promissory note that I pay back the debt with my good life.

"The only safe rule is to give more than we can spare." —C.S. Lewis, *Mere Christianity*.

Nature

The heavens declare the glory of God.
The expanse shows his handiwork.

Psalm 19:1, WEB

The Israelites found God in creation. They understood that the natural world they inhabited gave them not only a glimpse into God's glory and power, but also into God's laws. Night follows day, summer comes before winter, and death follows life. God's teachings were apparent to his desert children, and they praised God for such wisdom.

Lord, we confuse our days and nights, for we can make twenty-four-hour daylight. We live in jumbled seasons, flying in January to summer beaches and cranking up the air conditioning when summer swelters. We watch actors die in front of our eyes only to be reborn again in a new movie or TV drama. Our children live in virtual worlds directed by their own imaginations. In spite of all that we do to ignore or sidestep Your creation, You continue to offer us a world that engages our bodies, minds, and spirits. Help me to spend part of my days in Your real world, so that I can see You in this gift of creation and better understand Your laws and hopes for me. Like the Israelites, I praise You for Your wisdom and love.

Psalm 19 is said to be one of the inspirations for Joseph Haydn's oratorio *The Creation*.

Neighbor

Yahweh's law is perfect, restoring the soul.
Yahweh's testimony is sure, making wise the simple.
Yahweh's precepts are right, rejoicing the heart.
Yahweh's commandment is pure, enlightening the eyes.

Psalm 19:7–8, WEB

The psalmist reminds the faithful of God's just and perfect law, the 613 commands that guided every detail of Hebrew life. God taught them when and how to pray, what to eat, and how to plant their fields. Torah law shone a light onto the living and illuminated the widows and orphans, the old, and the poor, and it commanded the Hebrews to take care of each other. God's law showed them how to be each other's comfort in a difficult world.

With Your creative power, You populated this planet with a diverse array of people, and in Your goodness, You gave us rules to follow so we could live with each other. The poet Robert Frost wrote, "Good fences make good neighbors," but Your laws are not about separating people. Your laws help neighbors come together and live in harmony—don't lie, don't steal, don't commit adultery, and for God's sake, don't kill each other. We don't always follow Your laws, but they guide us in right living, as You wisely knew they would.

Christian author C.S. Lewis considered Psalm 19 to be "the greatest poem in the Psalter."

Networking

He who walks blamelessly does what is right,
and speaks truth in his heart;
He who doesn't slander with his tongue,
nor does evil to his friend,
nor casts slurs against his fellow man;

Psalm 15:2–3, WEB

The psalmist asks and answers an important question: Who shall live on God's holy hill? The answer is simple: Those who are righteous and who do not attack others with hurtful words and slander. A person of integrity lives with truth, and this person shall sojourn in God's tent.

It's challenging to navigate today's rapid-fire communications. My fingers tap out speedy replies to myriad friends and family, and experience has taught me that it's all too easy to text a terse slam instead of a civil comment. Like King Solomon who felt humbled by his responsibilities, I know networking can get me in over my head; but like the king who turned to You for wisdom, I also know I can turn to You for guidance as I craft the messages that travel through cyberspace at breakneck speed. You do not slow the pace of the communications, but Your presence reminds me that truth telling and kind regard for others must live in every message.

A wisdom psalm, Psalm 15 offers an honest, simple description of the person who will dwell with God.

Noise

Praise him with the sounding of the trumpet!
Praise him with harp and lyre!
Praise him with tambourine and dancing!
Praise him with stringed instruments and flute!

Psalm 150:3–4, WEB

The Israelites rocked out, putting their artistic muscle into praising God. They clanged cymbals, beat drums, blew horns, and plucked strings. They moved mouth, and hand, and feet in praise of their God. If they'd had electric guitars and snare drums, surely they would have employed them to send the din heavenward in honor of the Lord.

When the rhythms in my headphones rock me to a different beat, I am dancing with You. When the raucous sounds of the pop concert fill my ears, I know that even in that noisy crowd, I am close to You. When children march with drums and horns around the kitchen table, they are making happy sounds of prayer, even if they don't realize they are praying. Every moment of Your children's ear-splitting clatter praises You. If You help me to remember that the musical noise that infuses my life is a daily prayer in praise of You, I can smile knowing I am at my prayerful best when life is boisterous.

In most Bibles, Psalm 150 is the last psalm, a final shout-out of praise, or hallelujah.

People

Those who trust in the Lord are like Mount Zion,
which cannot be shaken but endures forever.
As the mountains surround Jerusalem,
so the Lord surrounds his people both now and forevermore.

Psalm 125:1–2, NIV

To those ascending the hills toward Jerusalem, the mountains' very presence reassures the Israelites. Yes, enemies once destroyed their temple. Yes, they were taken captive and exiled. What matters most, however, is that God's love endures. God's love is as strong and lasting as the mountains surrounding the holy city.

I often imagine You as my larger-than-life mom or dad. Sometimes I picture You tossing me gently into the air, as a mother does her toddler or a father his wriggling little girl. I know I'm not Your only child, and sometimes I struggle with having to remember that I'm part of a family that includes about 7 billion people. You, however, take being a mega-parent in stride. You surround all Your people, not as an army surrounds the enemy, but as a parent enfolds a child—lovingly, but sometimes with a gentle restraint. You are like unshakeable, enduring mountains encircling Your people's fragile bodies and wills, making us one with You, even when we sometimes act as if we want to wriggle free.

➻ **A copy of the *Bay Psalm Book*, the first book printed in North America, sold for $14.2 million in 2013.**

Popularity

Do not put your trust in princes,
in human beings, who cannot save.
Blessed are those whose help is the God of Jacob,
whose hope is in the Lord their God.

Psalm 146:3, 5, NIV

The psalmist trusts in God's kindness and generosity, so he can confidently tell the Israelites not to look to mere humans for their support and protection. The Israelites had suffered at the hands of many rulers; even some of their fellow Israelites had not always behaved well. As for God, he remained steadfast in his love.

God, because I know You love me and keep me in Your care, I can bypass the "in crowd" for any of its thoughts about what's popular or how I should live my life. Your words have taught me to measure myself by Your standards—be kind, be loving, be generous, care about others, and hold God close to my heart. With that wisdom, I don't need advice from those who see themselves as hip and who always feel obliged to give their opinions. I don't need compliments or criticisms from people who want to measure me against their standards. I can confidently say, "Thanks, but I'm okay. I'm tight with God."

For prayerful Jews, each day begins with the recitation of the last five psalms, starting with Psalm 146.

Poverty

I will bless her with abundant provisions;
her poor I will satisfy with food.
I will clothe her priests with salvation,
and her faithful people will ever sing for joy.

Psalm 132:15–16, NIV

When the Israelites sang on their way up to the temple, they remembered two important promises. First, they had promised God that they would revere him and follow his laws, because they knew their God was all they needed for a rich life. Second, God promised to care for those who honored him.

God, I'm fortunate, for I can buy what I need and have not known poverty. Since I've been little, Your words have taught me what You require of those who know abundance: share with others. When I hunger for things, You gently remind me to turn my desire for possessions into yearnings to live a more generous life. When I'm blue or bored and look to retail therapy for a quick fix, I can hear You say, "Turn toward others and help them." When my cravings for things surpass my gratefulness for what I have, I hear Your admonishment that if I seek only what money can buy, I will be truly needy; but if I share my abundance with others, I will be rich indeed.

Psalm 132, a messianic psalm, reaffirms God's choice of David as the right ruler to guide the Israelites.

Relationships

You have enclosed me behind and before,
And laid Your hand upon me.
Where can I go from Your Spirit?
Or where can I flee from Your presence?

Psalm 139:5, 7, NASB

The psalmist knows he can never escape God; for where he goes, God is also there. So, instead of trying to outsmart God and hide, the poet sings praises to an ever-present and all-knowing God, who keeps his eyes and his hand on him. The psalmist knows the answers to his questions about escape. He can never flee God. Thank God.

Like the psalmist, God, You boxed me in, and I'm glad You're behind me and before me and have given me no options but to turn to You. Why wouldn't I be glad? When two people are tight, they want to hang together, because joy and comfort flow from such togetherness. At first, God, knowing You saw everything I did and knew everything I thought made me nervous. Sometimes I even stopped talking to You, in hopes of being less obvious. Nevertheless, You kept Your hand and Your eyes on me, and now I want to post it on my Facebook wall—God and I are in a relationship.

On YouTube, the award-winning Christian musician Michael W. Smith recites Psalm 139 during a performance from his album *Worship*.

Retirement

Blessed is everyone who fears Yahweh,
who walks in his ways.
For you will eat the labor of your hands.
You will be happy, and it will be well with you.

Psalm 128:1-2, WEB

As they walked up the hillside to Jerusalem's temple, the Israelites sang their praises for God's blessings. They knew God's gifts weren't simply handouts. They had secured their blessings through obedience to God's holy laws, and they assured their own prosperity through the work of their hands. Life was good, because they collaborated with God for their own happiness.

I have worked hard, God, and I intend to work diligently until the day I feel free to retire; but work isn't the only thing that's had my commitment. I have tried to work on my relationship with You, and You have blessed me for my faithfulness and my efforts, as modest as they have been. I'm confident that my retirement will be comfortable, because I know each day on the job contributes to my secure tomorrows. I also know that as I store up treasures with You, my later years will be contented ones, for You are generous with Your blessings.

Because it spells out how to live a happy life, Psalm 128 is among the Wisdom Psalms.

Safety

Blessed are those whose strength is in you,
whose hearts are set on pilgrimage.

Psalm 84:5, NIV

Pilgrimages to the temple, though anticipated, were not easy expeditions in a desert. The Israelites put their hope in God, asking for the strength to go the distance in safety. They also knew that they needed God's strength to feel safe through their own life's journey.

God, You know I'm not a casual risk-taker, but when I've had to make a change or seek a new direction in my life, I've felt safe to strike out on that pilgrimage. I could take a chance, because You listened to my hemming and hawing and my what-ifs and maybes. From the big decisions in my life like jumping to a new job, or checking out a new city, or saying "I do," You were there making me feel secure about my future. Even the small gambles like speaking up for someone else, or striking up a conversation with a stranger, or even walking in a neighborhood where I didn't understand the language, You gave me courage. Your strength enriched my daily pilgrimage. God, I'm amazed that every day You offer me Your spiritual muscle, and every day that strength keeps me steadily walking into my life.

The psalms are written in the poetic form known as "free verse."

Self-confidence

I was small among my brothers,
and the youngest in my father's house.
I tended my father's sheep.

Psalm 151:1, NRSV

No one expected great things from David, the youngest of Jesse's eight sons and the smallest. He was a mere shepherd boy when Samuel anointed him as God's chosen one. The Lord saw in David the courage, intelligence, and faithfulness not only to defeat the terrorizing giant Goliath, but also to lead the great nation of Israel. Because he knew God chose him, David lived with the confidence that God was always by his side.

God, David was small, but he slew a giant, and people were amazed, but You weren't. Often people fail to notice each other's talents, because when they look only at what's on the outside, they miss the inside magic. On the outside, I may seem timid and unsure, but You see into my heart where I feel strong, and smart, and ready to tackle anything. Thank You, God, for seeing my potential even when others might pass me by. Because You believe in me, I can believe in myself.

Though not in the traditional Psalter, Psalm 151 is an original Hebrew psalm pointing to the story of David and Goliath.

Setbacks

Who remembered us in our low estate;
for his loving kindness endures forever;
And has delivered us from our adversaries;
for his loving kindness endures forever:

Psalm 136:23–24, WEB

Captivity and exile in Babylon took the Israelites to new lows, and they suffered in body and spirit. Nevertheless, God remained faithful and those who turned to him found comfort. When he delivered them back to their homeland, they chanted as if in one voice about God's everlasting love, and joyously sang the litany refrain that his loving kindness endures forever.

Sometimes my setbacks hold me captive in the hard land of disappointment. Discouragement may weigh my spirits down, but You remain unflagging in Your faithfulness to me. During my setbacks, when I believed my luck had permanently changed for the worst, You bolstered me up so that I never completely lost faith in myself. I know that You never consider me too small or too unworthy for Your ceaseless care. My worries and struggles never escape Your notice. You support me through my impediments, help me step over my barriers, and continue to be my best cheerleader. Your love never ends.

Psalm 136 is chanted at the end of the Passover meal, as Jesus might have done at the Last Supper.

Sexuality

Behold, children are a heritage of Yahweh.
The fruit of the womb is his reward.

Psalm 127:3, WEB

For the Israelites, children were a sign that God had blessed a husband and wife or a nation. The psalmist mentions children as numerous as arrows in a quiver, for he believes that through children, God gives both blessing and security.

I confess, God, I have had many a time during sex, when I didn't want to think about having children. I wanted to enjoy the moment and not ponder a future that included responsibilities and sacrifices for children. I even can recall some scary times when I feared I might become a parent before I was ready. Then, God, You blessed me with my first child, and Your gift of sexuality and of my baby suddenly connected deep within my heart. In Your great generosity, You have made it possible for my body to luxuriate in passion, and through that passion with and for another to create a new life that has become the center of my life. How great You are.

Some believe King Solomon, David's beloved son, authored Psalm 127, a testament to the blessings of children.

Sleep

You have put more joy in my heart
than they have when their grain and new wine abound.
I will both lie down and sleep in peace,
for You alone, Lord, make me live in safety.

Psalm 4:7–8, HCSB

As the shadows gather at day's end, the psalmist sings a sweet, simple prayer to God. He remarks that not only will he lie down, but also he will fall asleep peacefully. Here's an untroubled man, a man who places so much trust in God that even if his enemy slept nearby, no fears would make him toss and turn.

Sometimes I share my bed with worries, and sometimes I replay conversations hoping my imagination will create a happier outcome than the one I experienced. When my mind is too active with the day's troubles and my heart too weary from the day's struggles, I know I can turn to You. I let my imagination take me to Your shoulder where I nestle my head and feel Your comforting presence. I picture Your arm around my shoulder squeezing me with Your reassurance. In those moments, I fall fast asleep, for no coverlet is softer or safer than You.

➤ **Psalm 4 is often seen as an evening psalm, because it is the poet's prayer before falling asleep.**

Solitude

I will say of the Lord,
He is my refuge and my fortress:
my God; in him will I trust.

Psalm 91:2, KJV

In time of danger, confusion, or atonement, the Israelites fled to the temple, for it was a place of refuge against enemies and human failings. As they sang their song of trust, they found reassurance in God's home and in God's presence.

God, You shelter me, not from any enemies but from the craziness of my own life. I don't always seek You in prayer, but when I remember to whisper even a quick, "Hi, God," I can feel Your soothing presence. You urge me to take a breath and slow down and to stop watching the clock and just hang out a bit with You. In Your wisdom, You step in and become my buffer from life's bustle and from the cacophony of voices and opinions that saturate my days. Time with You is so reassuring and reminds me that stillness and solitude replenish my spirit. I need to find more moments of quiet with You, so let's get on each other's day planners and do this more often.

In Hebrew, this psalm uses four different names for the Divine: Elyon (Most High), Shaddai (Almighty), YHWH (Lord), and Elohim (God).

Strangers

The Lord raises up those who are bowed down;
The Lord loves the righteous;
The Lord protects the strangers;
He supports the fatherless and the widow,
But He thwarts the way of the wicked.

Psalm 146:8b–9, NASB

The psalmist extols God's compassionate nature, for God consistently reaches out to protect the most vulnerable. The Israelites understood that women without husbands, children without fathers, and those traveling through unfamiliar territory were at the mercy of others. God stands between them and evildoers.

I live in a land of new arrivals, and daily I pass people who do not look like me. Their accents broadcast that they were not born here. Their clothing publicizes that they are aliens. Unfamiliar cooking smells waft from their windows, and they worship in places I have never entered. The strangeness of these visitors might unsettle me, God, were it not for Your example. You commanded the Israelites to shelter the stranger; therefore, I must not fear people simply because they are foreign to me. Your words tell me that strangers are my guests in need of generous hospitality. You urge me to look their way and to let my smile say, "Welcome."

The last five psalms, which include Psalm 146, are called the Hallelujah Psalms, because they begin and end with "Hallelujah."

Strength

Praise ye the Lord.
Praise God in his sanctuary:
praise him in the firmament of his power.
Praise him for his mighty acts:
praise him according to his excellent greatness.

Psalm 150:1–2, KJV

In this psalm, the closing song of the Book of Psalms, the psalmist unabashedly praises God and acknowledges his saving strength. While other psalms include various verses of praise to the God of Israel, all of Psalm 150 is an unabashed song of praise.

God, You are omnipresent. Your sanctuary is not confined to a synagogue or church. Instead, Your sanctuary surrounds me, whether I'm sending a sensitive text, making an unpopular decision, trying to feel brave on a long walk home alone, or just trying to hold my own in a tough conversation. You strengthen my footsteps, firm my voice, and clear my head. In Your omnipotence, You lend Your strength to all of Your creation, including me. Therefore, no matter where I stand, I stand on Your holy ground, and no matter what I am called on to overcome, I know I can call on Your strength to see me through.

Some scholars think Psalm 150 celebrated the dedication of the temple in Jerusalem—the Israelites' most holy sanctuary.

Terrorism

Therefore will not we fear,
though the earth be removed,
and though the mountains be carried
into the midst of the sea;

Psalm 46:2, KJV

A witness to great social and political strife, the psalmist offers poetic images of quaking ground and mountains disappearing into the oceans. Clearly he lives in troubling times, but his song's refrain leaves room for hope: "The Lord of hosts is with us: the God of Jacob is our refuge."

I can avoid news of the latest acts of terrorism by canceling my newspapers, turning off my television, or refusing to read news feeds on my iPhone. I could pretend that the craziness literally exploding in this world is not my concern, but clearly I would be the crazy one to ignore such hate and the suffering it brings. So instead of my distress, God, I choose to turn to You with gratefulness, because I believe You will not ignore such deadly strife. Even as I pray, I know Your words and wisdom, Your admonishments against the violent, and Your rewards to those who seek Your path surely will hold sway in terror-ridden lands.

Psalm 46 inspired Martin Luther to compose "A Mighty Fortress Is Our God."

Theft

He lurks in secret as a lion in his ambush.
He lies in wait to catch the helpless.
He catches the helpless,
when he draws him in his net.

Psalm 10:9, WEB

The psalmist notes what good people everywhere know—evildoers lurk around every corner and prey on the weak. The psalmist doesn't name the wicked ones; they could be enemies, false accusers, or thieves waiting to steal something under the dark of night. In the face of evil, the psalmist's advice is consistent: trust in God.

I'm not blameless of theft simply because I do not take someone's possessions. God, I praise You for teaching me how to place the helpless in the bigger picture and to protect them from robbers. Your words teach me not to remain silent when I know a thief has used fists to fleece a woman of her self-respect. I must not look the other way when a caregiver steals an elder's dignity or a bully robs a child of self-confidence. I cannot be deaf when I hear gossip that strips away another's privacy or holds the person up to ridicule. I am blameless of thievery only if I am vigilant for thieves who would deprive the weak of their inner peace.

Many ponder whether Psalms 9 and 10 were once one psalm, with both reflecting on the power of evildoers.

Time

The eyes of all wait for you.
You give them their food in due season.
You open your hand,
and satisfy the desire of every living thing.

Psalm 145:15–16, WEB

This psalm sings out its praises to God, declaring him awesome, powerful, and generous. With his perpetual love, God attends to his children's needs, knowing just the right time in which to bestow much needed help or blessing.

I've heard all the *time* clichés. I know we can "kill time," "make time," and "save time." "Time stands still" and "time flies," but the only time really worth noting, God, is Your time. The season of God surpasses any trite expression people may wish to fashion, for You are generous with Your time and wise in knowing just the right time to challenge or care for Your children. I've had times, God, when I've pleaded, "Enough. I can't handle anymore," but You knew I could. I've begged, "Please, now," and in Your wisdom You knew, "Not yet." I'm blessed to have a heavenly parent who knows by the minute when the time is right to test me or bless me.

All of Psalm 145, a hymn of praise, is recited three times daily in the synagogue.

Violence

Mark the perfect man, and see the upright,
for there is a future for the man of peace.

Psalm 37:37, WEB

The psalmist presses the faithful: Don't be discouraged by the seeming success of the wicked. Look at those things that at first seem to flourish for evildoers but then reveal the story of their destruction. Lush grasses perish in the heat of summer, just as captors lose their hold, and enemies pass away. God's people, however, live on.

Stories of violence are everywhere—men against women, race against race, and Jews, Christians, and Muslims against each other. I hear of parents who have harmed their children, strangers who pull guns on each other, and profiteers who would enslave the poor and helpless for their own gain. This appalling onslaught could crush my spirit, until I remember You, and Your words point me toward sanity. I praise You for Your consistent message—love others as I have loved you. Treat others as you wish to be treated. Today may be filled with violence, but the future—maybe as near as tomorrow—will stand with people of peace. You have declared that evil will not be victorious.

The Sermon on the Mount echoes the sentiments found in Psalm 37—faithfulness and goodness will triumph.

War

O let the nations be glad and sing for joy:
for thou shalt judge the people righteously,
and govern the nations upon earth. Selah.

Psalm 67:4, KJV

The psalmist believes that if God blesses the Israelites, then their homeland will be an example of justice and righteousness; therefore, a blessing to the world. With the addition of the word *selah,* he asks those singing the psalm to pause. Perhaps the singers literally need to stop and take a breath, but perhaps they need to pause and ponder the psalm's message: God governs the nations.

God, when people collectively feel at ease and joyous in each other's company, they are less likely to fight each other. When people can agree that the duty of all nations is to treat their citizens fairly and to behave righteously with their neighbors, we will have no need for war. God, when people pause and take a moment to praise You, they have one less moment to fight with each other—at home, at church, on the street, or across the seas in another land. If I take moments throughout my day to pause and praise You, perhaps I will be less disagreeable with others, and my heart will know a greater peace.

Psalm 67 may have been sung at Sukkoth, or Feast of Tabernacles, a harvest festival that required a temple pilgrimage.

Work

I removed his shoulder from the burden.
His hands were freed from the basket.
You called in trouble, and I delivered you.

Psalm 81:6–7a, WEB

The Israelites will never forget the moment when Moses lifted the burden of their enslavement. No longer would their shoulders ache from the oppression of carrying baskets of clay to Pharaoh's brick works. Their backs would no longer bleed under the lash. Using the determination and faith of the humble shepherd Moses, God delivered them.

Moses led his people across the Red Sea, but it wasn't his idea; it was Yours. Throughout time, You have reached into our hearts to nurture the notion that we are called to carry each other's burdens. The person who shovels a neighbor's snow bends and lifts to Your work, as do the cooks who carry casseroles to those burdened by grief. You remind us to ask, "May I help?" or "May I carry that for you?" Sometimes You call us to labor with our hearts instead of our bodies. Then You nudge us to ask, "Are you all right? Should I sit with you?" You have taught us that we are Your eyes, and hands, and feet on this earth, and when we carry another's load, You are our loving overseer.

Likely Psalm 81 was sung at the Feast of the Tabernacles, a joyous celebration remembering God's protection in the wilderness.

Worry

My soul waits for the Lord
More than the watchmen for the morning;
Indeed, more than the watchmen for the morning.

Psalm 130:6, NASB

A nightly spectacle in the Hebrews' desert towns, the watchman leaned sleepily against walkway walls or stood silently in doorways. Rarely did a watchman do anything but wait. Remembering these solitary figures, the psalmist comforts his own anxieties. Morning will come unbidden to every watchman. Night is never forever; it ends with the sun, and so too will the Israelites' worries.

Like a watchman who simply stands and waits, I worry. I do nothing, I plan nothing, and I can change nothing, so I worry. Weather, family traveling on the highway, news of terrorism in the Middle East or famine in Somalia sets me to-handwringing, and I wait, and I worry. You reach into my anxious moments and remind me that the watchman's wait will end at dawn. The rose and orange glow of Your rising sun will banish the night's shadows and glooms. You, Lord, are my hope, for I know my worries can rest in You. Remembering Your presence, I can stop holding my breath.

Psalm 130 inspired poems entitled "De Profundis" by such poets as C.S. Lewis, Christina Rossetti, and Alfred Tennyson.

Thanksgiving

GOD, THANKS SO MUCH

Aging

For you are my hope, Lord Yahweh;
my confidence from my youth.

Psalm 71:5, WEB

The Hebrews knew the inspiring stories of young men who succeeded because they or others placed their faith in God. Moses was set adrift in the bull rushes, David slew Goliath and went on to become king, and Joseph was sold into slavery, only to prosper and save his family from starvation. Each came to place his trust in God as he grew into manhood, and they lifted their voices to God for his steadfast love.

God, I haven't always turned to You. To be honest, when I was a kid, I often forgot You were near. However, as I grow older and I hope wiser, I am grateful for Your ongoing tender care. In my tears, I turn more to You for comfort. In my confusion, I know I can look to You for wisdom. When I feel the joys of success, I'm now old enough to know I didn't achieve something all by myself—I did it with Your help. I'm now confident that You have never left my side and will continue to walk with me even as I grow old and face new challenges. Who says older people can't get smarter?

This psalm carries the title "Humble Prayer in the Time of Old Age."

Death

As the deer pants for streams of water,
so my soul pants for you, my God.
My soul thirsts for God, for the living God.
When can I go and meet with God?

Psalm 42:1–2, NIV

The psalmist misses worshipping in the temple and feeling especially close to God within that sacred space. So great is his longing for God that he compares himself to a deer thirsting for a refreshing stream. Perhaps the psalmist is miles away from Jerusalem, and in his sadness, he cries out for the comfort of being in God's holy space.

Death should be a sad thing, and yet I am overflowing with thanksgiving. Death may have broken my heart, but my grief can't bury my gratefulness, because I know that the person I loved and lost longed to be home with You. How can I want to hold onto a soul seeking Your presence? Would I really want to deny a spirit refreshment in Your arms? The answer is "no." In spite of my tears, I give thanks that my loved one has reached a longed-for destination—You. I take comfort in remembering that, for the person I loved and lost, death was not the end but an anticipated goal. Thus, my sorrow eases and so does my sadness.

Maskil psalms teach a lesson, and Psalm 42 instructs the listener to joyfully long for God.

Decisions

Yahweh's voice is powerful.
Yahweh's voice is full of majesty.
Yahweh's voice strikes with flashes of lightning.
Yahweh's voice shakes the wilderness.
Yahweh shakes the wilderness of Kadesh.

Psalm 29:4, 7–8, WEB

Perhaps a powerful thunderstorm has pushed the poet's thoughts toward God. He hears the deep roll of God's voice high in the heavens and watches in awe and perhaps fear as lightning bolts punctuate God's power and majesty. Small in comparison to the enveloping storm coming in from the Mediterranean Sea, he imagines God's voice resonating across the Promised Land, swinging north to Lebanon and then south to the wilderness of Kadesh.

I love to watch a powerful summer storm move in. Even before the rains drench me, thunder hits my ears and lightning bolts dance in the distance. Like the psalmist, I too think of You when thunder booms, for those rumbles remind me of Your powerful voice. I'm grateful that when I have tough decisions to make, Your voice never wavers. Your directions are clear, Your desires unmistakable. Life is filled with alternatives, and sometimes deciding among them overwhelms me. So, when life offers confusing choices, I pause and listen for Your firm and loving voice.

Scholars note that the imagery in Psalm 29 reflects the poetry from a neighboring Canaanite song honoring a powerful god.

Depression

He refreshes my soul.
He guides me along the right paths
for his name's sake.

Psalm 23:3, NIV

The paths that cut through a meadow are many, for sheep and shepherds alike beat down the grasses and set the eye to following any number of tramped trails. The psalmist offers assurance that the shepherd not only knows the right path, but he also will guide his sheep to comfort and safety. They may not know their way, but he does.

I was lost and weighed down and didn't know which way to turn. Caught in the revolving door of my own sadness, I couldn't step out into calm, and then You rescued me. Like some broad-shouldered shepherd, You scooped me up and draped my weary soul around Your neck. You carried me to safety and far away from the dangers of depression. In Your wisdom, You knew that family, laughter, friends, and meaningful days would refresh my spirits, and You set me on those paths. Today I lift my face into the sunshine and whisper, "Thank you."

Psalm 23 often is sung or read at Jewish and Christian funeral services.

Disappointment

For You do not delight in sacrifice, otherwise I would give it;
You are not pleased with burnt offering.
The sacrifices of God are a broken spirit;
A broken and a contrite heart, O God, You will not despise.

Psalm 51:16–17, NASB

The sinner, deeply disappointed in himself, knows what will make him right with God. He rejects a burnt offering—the traditional way to seek God's favor. Instead, he looks deep within himself and ponders his broken spirit and how to rebuild his link to God. Perhaps with tears, certainly with prayerful lament, he imagines offering up his crushed spirit. "I'm sorry," he cries. "Mend me, God."

I can admit it now—I was a bully in school. Steeped in insecurity, I called others names. Worried no one would like me, I assailed the unpopular kids: "You can't sit with us," I sneered. "Are you queer?" I taunted. It was never about them, God. It was always about my lack of confidence. I see that now, and I feel disappointment in my younger self. I also see that my embarrassment about the past makes me wiser in the present. Thank You for showing me that when I feel broken is when I am closer to forgiving myself, as You have forgiven me so many times.

One of the seven penitential psalms, Psalm 51 is recited during Ash Wednesday services in many Christian churches.

Distractions

Surely I have behaved and quieted myself,
as a child that is weaned of his mother:
my soul is even as a weaned child.

Psalm 131:2, KJV

The psalmist, possibly King David, has found peace and contentment. He asks the listener to picture a baby about to suckle at its mother's breast. Squirming and agitated, the infant roots for its heart's desire. The weaned child, however, no longer fusses and wriggles; it sits contentedly on its mother's lap. So, too, the psalmist finds himself resting comfortably with God, no longer fretting for nor distracted by the worldly things that have lured away his attentions.

Thank God I'm past the time where my ego drones incessantly: feed me, praise me, take care of my self-esteem, and make me feel important. Gone are those lengthy "To Do" lists that measured my significance. I'm no longer twisted in knots and distracted by who's succeeding, who has more cool stuff, who gets more invitations, and whose partners are sexier. I'm not fueling a slow burn about someone who I thought had snubbed me, and I no longer obsess about being on a fast track to success. Thankfully, Your words have taught me how to rest quietly in You.

When the New Testament refers to verses from the Old Testament, forty percent of those references are to psalms.

Dreams

This is the day which the Lord hath made;
we will rejoice and be glad in it.

Psalm 118:24, KJV

The psalmist has created a royal song of thanksgiving for the king to sing as he enters the temple and offers his grateful prayers to God. Likely, he comes to the temple after the exile in Babylonia. For him and the Israelites, this offering of praise sets their hearts to glorifying the God, who has fulfilled their hopes and dreams for deliverance.

I dream about my tomorrows and how life will be, but today is the gift You have given me right now. If I rejoice in the greatness of that gift—the people, the work before me, and the satisfaction I will feel in these twenty-four hours—then I am gratefully living in and using Your gift. My dreams about the future tell me where I want to go, but dreaming alone won't get me where I want to see myself next year or in five years. Using the talents I have today and growing the happiness You provide right now, in these moments, will help me realize my dreams. Thank You, God, for giving me the ability to dream and the power and opportunity to make those dreams come true.

Psalm 118 is in the exact middle of the Bible and is quoted twelve times in the New Testament.

Environment

He makes the clouds his chariot.
He walks on the wings of the wind.
He makes his messengers winds;
his servants flames of fire.

Psalm 104:3b-4, WEB

To the Israelites, everything in nature spoke of God's glory. The psalmist saw God in chariot clouds commanding messengers of wind and servants of fire. Nature knelt before God, ready to serve and to be of service. The natural world and God were one.

God, I'm thankful that You take charge of our planet and have its elements at Your command, because I worry about our Mother Earth. I'm uneasy about whether she can survive the human assault on her air, and waters, and land. I know that even when humans try to be responsible, their sheer numbers challenge the earth's resources. I ask myself, "How long before the environmental dangers become too much?" Then I pause and remember that nature recognizes You as its creator, and You have always cared for Your masterpiece. I may not understand Earth's complex systems, but I'm thankful that You do. Help me to be grateful for Your steadfast care of Earth and for Your guidance in how we might share in her protection.

In the Roman Catholic Church, Psalm 104 is the responsorial psalm sung during the Easter Vigil on Holy Saturday.

Faith

Blessed are those who have regard for the weak;
the Lord delivers them in times of trouble.
The Lord protects and preserves them—
they are counted among the blessed in the land—
he does not give them over to the desire of their foes.

Psalm 41:1–2, NIV

The poet offers a lesson in God's love. Take care of the weak, the sick, and the troubled among you, and God will protect and preserve you. If you are among the needy, God will bless you and protect you from your enemies. God blesses both those in need and those who step forward to care for the weak.

If I were to count the weak and needy of this world, I would have to include myself in those numbers. I enjoy few luxuries. In comparison to many others, however, my struggles are small and so are my successes. Yet, You call others to regard me, to tend me when I am ill and to look out for me should trouble come. In turn, You charge me with opening my eyes to the needs and sufferings of others. What a gift You've given us. You charge us by our faith to be mindful of others, and because of our faith, You will be mindful of us and bestow Your blessing.

The Roman Catholic Church includes Verse 2 in a prayer during its invocation for the pope.

Family

For the Lord is good
and his love endures forever;
his faithfulness continues through all generations.

Psalm 100:5, NIV

As they entered the temple, the Israelites sang this psalm, which has only five verses, because they were overflowing with thanksgiving for God. They knew they were God's chosen ones for eternity, and they offered their sacrifices in gratitude for God's faithfulness.

I love my family, God. Each one, from the squirming babes to the aged, touches my heart. Each has required some sacrifices, because when you love someone, you spend your time, your energy, and your money on that person. You know I also sacrifice some peace of mind, because who doesn't worry about family? I have such hopes for them, such dreams. Then one day, I know I'll die and leave them. Because of You and Your ceaseless love, I do not worry about who will watch over them. The ones I've hugged and those yet to be born will forever be in Your care. Thanks, God. I breathe easier knowing that my family is Yours for eternity.

Using the tune "Old Hundredth," which this psalm inspired, William Kethe wrote "All People that on Earth Do Dwell."

Friends

Let the righteous strike me,
it is kindness;
let him reprove me,
it is like oil on the head;
don't let my head refuse it;
Yet my prayer is always against evil deeds.

Psalm 141:5, WEB

The wise person knows that a good friend will tell him the truth, even if the truth hurts. The psalmist clearly is a wise person, for he's willing to face tough words and corrections if they'll help him to be a better person.

Thanks, God, for my friends, the people who see me through tough times and good times. They know me, and because they do, I trust them to tell me the truth and to have my best interests at heart. My good friends won't let me act like a fool—at least not a second time. They'll tell me if I've been a jerk and accept my apology. They've even been known to tell me gently when they thought I wasn't taking good care of myself. Sometimes, God, I think You've given me such good friends so they can give me the messages I don't always hear You send my way.

Verse 5 sounds like a repetition of Proverbs 27:6, which advises, "Faithful are the wounds of a friend" (KJV).

Happiness

Enter into his gates with thanksgiving,
and into his courts with praise:
be thankful unto him,
and bless his name.

Psalm 100:4, KJV

The psalmist, overjoyed by God's goodness, can't wait to rush through the temple gates and into God's sanctuary. On his lips, he sings a short hymn of thanksgiving, which he offers up to God with a full heart.

Happiness fills my life. Sure, I've had my share of "blue" days, but in the balance of things, my life definitely tilts toward a bounty of small joys. God, thanks for the countless smile-makers You send my way. You tune my ears to good news, the ice cream truck, fun music, and laughter. You point my feet toward the night sidewalk where I find the gift of a star-lit sky. You alert my nose to the smell of roses and fill my arms with huggable children. I feel cuddly blankets on my shoulders at night and wet doggie kisses on my face in the morning. These delights fill my life. Help me to keep a thankful heart so that, like the psalmist, I am eager to spill over with gratitude.

The hymn melody "Old Hundredth" takes its name from Psalm 100, the only psalm inscribed as "a psalm of thanksgiving."

Health

Yea, though I walk through the valley of the shadow of death,
I will fear no evil:
for thou art with me;
thy rod and thy staff they comfort me.

Psalm 23:4, KJV

The Hebrews knew that the sheep in the field were in danger. Wolves could gobble them up; thieves could snatch them away. If they became separated from their flock, they could lose their security. Lucky the sheep that had a stalwart shepherd who stood ready to defend his sheep and to carry them home if they strayed.

My health is bad, and some days I feel the darkness of worry close in on me. This illness is an evil that has seeped into my bones. It robs me of my strength and my patience and in exchange gives me pain. Then in my bleak moments, my shepherd arrives to give me courage. Thank You for being my comfort during these hard days and long nights. Thank You for being with me, for holding tightly to my hand and leading me through this dark valley. I do not want to get lost, and I'm grateful that You have not let go of Your ailing lamb.

Likely Psalm 23 is the most well known of the psalms and among those most often recited.

Home

The trees of the Lord are well watered,
the cedars of Lebanon that he planted.
There the birds make their nests;
the stork has its home in the junipers.
The high mountains belong to the wild goats;
the crags are a refuge for the hyrax.

Psalm 104:16-18, NIV

The Israelites praised God for His glorious creation, singing their thanksgiving for his marvelous plan. God made the earth perfectly and thought of everything for His people.

God, because of You, I have "Home Sweet Home" everywhere I go. I've got the four walls and roof that I call "mine," but You've given me so much more. I love my neighborhood with familiar faces to wave to and dogs to pet. Thanks for planting me there; it's a perfect fit. I walk to my favorite pew at church, scoot down Aisle 3 at the grocery store for cereal, and follow well-known streets to friends and family. Even my desk at work beckons a "welcome" to me. Thanks to You, I feel at home everywhere that I go. My contentment comes from knowing You have placed me right where I need and want to be.

During morning services, observant Jews recite all of Psalm 104.

Loneliness

God sets the lonely in families.
He brings out the prisoners with singing,
but the rebellious dwell in a sun-scorched land.

Psalm 68:6, WEB

The psalmist opens this hymn with words Moses prayed, "Rise up, Lord, and let thine enemies be scattered;" (Nm10:35, KJV). The poet wants the prayerful to remember their journey through the desert with God, even as they journey into the temple carrying the Ark of the Covenant. He also wants them to find comfort in a God who protects widows and orphans and who stands with the lonely, whether desolate in spirit or circumstance.

Who hasn't been lonely? I've known brief, forlorn moments, but also long strings of lonesome days. Thankfully, You came and released me from the imprisonment of a sad heart and the constricted thinking that could have kept me from seeing the potential for joy in my life. You softened my loneliness with the gift of family—both the family I was born into and the family I fashioned from loving friends and colleagues. Loneliness can take us captive and chain us to regrets and sorrow, but I have learned if I surrender my lonesomeness to God, You will set me free.

Psalm 68, with its obscure vocabulary and complex themes, is regarded as the most difficult psalm to translate and understand.

Money

Trust not in oppression,
and become not vain in robbery:
if riches increase, set not your heart upon them.

Psalm 62:10, KJV

The psalmist seems to speak to the faithful from personal experience. Likely, he has known oppressive rulers or has been fooled by tricksters, who smiled as they pinched his purse. Most certainly, he has met nobles who valued riches more than their honor. Life has taught the poet that fleeting things like power and wealth have no value compared to the steadfastness of God.

The daily news has taught me that the pursuit of riches leads to grief. Ponzi schemers dead-end in prison and the deceived in regret. Housing market scams lead to bailouts and families' homes in foreclosure. However, long before CNN reporters, Your Gospels taught consistent lessons and Your words came through clearly: Don't put great stock in riches. Don't desire the luxuries of the world at the expense of your soul; and beware of greed, for it will harm your neighbor and distract you from God. Your words proved true. I'm thankful Your voice was louder than the shills hawking get-rich schemes, and I'm grateful that those words taught me to want an honest life more than I want money.

In Temple worship, a cantor would chant the psalm along with a priestly chorus.

Nature

For every beast of the forest is mine,
and the cattle upon a thousand hills.
I know all the fowls of the mountains:
and the wild beasts of the field are mine.
for the world is mine, and the fulness thereof.

Psalm 50:10–11, 12b, KJV

The psalmist reminds the faithful that everything that creeps and leaps, runs, swims, flies, and crawls already belongs to God. In good faith, the Israelites have given God their countless offerings of fatted calves and bleating goats, but the psalmist wonders: Can we really give to God what already belongs to the creator?

God, what amazes me is that everything You created, You generously share with all Your children. You may already own all that lives in this world, yet You are never covetous or tightfisted. You make us believe that this life-giving gift of our world is truly ours to enjoy and use. You ask no price, no rent—only our appreciation. As I step into each day, I want to remember that I am stepping into a gift that is mine to treasure and for which I can only say, "thank you," from a full heart.

Psalm 50 is seen as God's lesson on true worship: Bring me your loving heart and sincere prayer.

Neighbor

But it is good for me to come close to God.
I have made the Lord Yahweh my refuge,
that I may tell of all your works.

Psalm 73:28, WEB

Throughout his psalm, the poet struggles with one of life's hard lessons: the godless seem to do well, while those who obey God's commandments struggle to survive. The psalmist wants to cry out, "Not fair," but by the end of his musings, he does an about-face. He decides that what others suffer, carry out, or do not have is irrelevant. His own close relationship with God will determine his life and his eternal success.

Thank You for giving me the answer to the Gospel question, "Who is my neighbor?" I'm grateful that Your guidance was so clear and unequivocal—everyone is my neighbor and everyone deserves my watchful care and regard. I often miss the mark and sometimes struggle to feel neighborly to those I perceive as smug or rude, boastful or entitled. I've often wanted to cross the street or walk in the opposite direction rather than encounter someone heading my way who looks grubby or who sports an array of tattoos. I know, however, that when I put appearances and behaviors aside and think "neighbor," I find myself feeling closer to others and to You.

Psalm 73, considered one of the Wisdom Psalms, is the first psalm in Book Three of the Psalter.

Networking

That person is like a tree
planted by streams of water,
which yields its fruit in season
and whose leaf does not wither—
whatever they do prospers.

Psalm 1:3, NIV

The Israelites lived in a semi-arid land. They knew that to grow well and produce fruit, a tree needs to be near water, its roots networking down into the source of life. The psalmist also knew that God is a source of life, and those who networked into God would prosper.

God, I am thankful for the networks in my life that root me deeply into family, friends, and community, and I'm grateful to have my electronic devices that keep me connected to all of these. Within seconds, I can hear someone's voice, see the faces of loved ones, and read their thoughts on everything from politics to potty training. How can my heart wither when, at any moment, I'm able to fill myself up with those I love? Help me to remember that the many networks in my life enrich me and that these connections are reminders of my ongoing bond to You.

Psalm 1 leads off the collection of the Book of Psalms, which officially includes 150 psalms.

Noise

Make a joyful noise unto God, all ye lands:

Psalm 66:1, KJV

The Israelites had much to be thankful for. God delivered them from their enemies and settled them in a homeland. In their gratitude, they made joyful noises of "thanks" to God, and their psalms of appreciation could be heard throughout the lands.

Lord, You greeted the Israelites' noise of trumpet and harp, voices and cymbals with joy. The noises in my life also make me smile—voices clamoring with excitement and the music pouring from my ear buds put a spring in my step. The honking horns and shouts of people reaffirm that I live in community; I am not alone. I am connected to others—to their joys as well as to their sorrows. The minute-by-minute noises of my life confirm that I am alive in this world and able to partake in the abundant life that surrounds me. Help me to remember to be thankful for life's hubbub, because every bit of noise booms with the truth that You have given me life in a bustling world that perpetually sends its noises heavenward in thanksgiving.

In the Greek Bible, Psalm 66 is called "A Psalm of the Resurrection" and may be recited at Easter services.

People

Oh come, let's worship and bow down.
Let's kneel before Yahweh, our Maker, for he is our God.
We are the people of his pasture, and the sheep in his care.
Today, oh that you would hear his voice!

Psalm 95:6–7, WEB

The Israelites were bound to God and to each other by the 613 laws God gave to Moses. No matter their squabbles with each other; they were united through their shared covenant with Yahweh. No matter their occasional lapses with God, they were God's sheep, and God was their shepherd. As the psalmist calls them to worship, his words remind them that they and God share deeply interwoven connections of love and duty.

No matter who we are or where we come from, God, we're all children in Your creation. Like sheep in the meadows, we depend on You and we share common ground with each other. When You called us to care for one another, I'm grateful You embraced everyone. I don't get the option to scratch enemies off my Love List or reject people on the street who make me nervous. I don't get to shun those whose opinions differ from mine or whose appearance says they are not like me. Thankfully, You left no wiggle room—Love one another as I have loved you.

In the Jewish tradition, Psalm 95 is among the psalms read on Friday evening at the start of Shabbat.

Popularity

Oh clap your hands, all you nations.
Shout to God with the voice of triumph!
The princes of the peoples are gathered together,
the people of the God of Abraham.
For the shields of the earth belong to God. He is greatly exalted!

Psalm 47:1, 9, WEB

The psalmist's poem harkens to a coronation that includes the crowd's jubilation and the ruler's majestic ascent to the throne. Joyously the faithful declare, "Yahweh is king," for he rules over heaven and earth. He is higher than even the earthly princes; therefore, the peoples of all nations look to God alone as the most high.

Music, literature, art, architecture, history books, and today's twenty-four-hour newscasts make it clear, God, that through recorded time, billions of people have paid You homage and continue to call out Your name. People in churches, mosques, temples, and synagogues daily worship the ruler of all; through songs and supplications, they call out to You. I suspect You don't care about popularity contests, but I'm heartened that You have a large, international fan base. Your message across time and nations is consistent: Love one another; take care of one another. I take heart knowing that Your popularity moves this world toward a better place as people everywhere seek to live out Your decree.

In Catholic churches, Psalm 47 is sung on Palm Sunday, when palms are distributed to the faithful.

Poverty

He will regard the prayer of the destitute,
and not despise their prayer.
For he hath looked down from the height of his sanctuary;
from heaven did the Lord behold the earth;

Psalm 102:17, 19, KJV

The psalmist's poem starts with "a prayer for the lowly when he grows faint." The beleaguered Hebrews were in distress and faint of heart, for in exile they had endured a prolonged separation from their homeland. When they sent their prayers heavenward, God heard them and restored their land and their spirits.

Thank you, God, for hearing Your children's sorrows, especially the miseries from those who have so little—too little food, inadequate housing, and not enough money to care for their families. You have sent them food pantries, donations to help with utility bills, subsidized housing and childcare, and compassionate employers. To those whose spirits are impoverished because of illness, losses, or depression, You have delivered listening neighbors, attentive caregivers, and mental health professionals and social workers. In Your kindness, You answer the prayers of the destitute through the helping hands and hearts of those listening to Your voice and willing to be Your ears, eyes, and hands on Earth.

All the psalms speak to or about God—his laws, power, and steadfast love for the Israelites.

Relationships

Give thanks to the Lord, for He is good;
His faithful love endures forever.

Psalm 118:1, HCSB

A powerful song of thanksgiving, this psalm opens with two deeply held beliefs: God is good and God is faithful. Likely, the Israelites sang this psalm as a litany upon entering the temple, with the believers repeating in unison, "His faithful love endures forever." Generations later, they said this prayer of grateful praise near the close of the Seder meal.

God, You have given me the gift of so many life-affirming relationships. They fill me with love and nourish my heart. I'm also grateful that through Your own example, You have modeled how I should be in relationship with others. I must be faithful, and I must hang in there for a long time—especially when it's hard. I must help to shoulder my loved ones' burdens and stand near, even if all I do is listen. I must forgive, no matter how often, and I must let those I love know that I believe in them. All these things You have done for me, and with You as my gentle teacher, I can now grow loving relationships with others and continue the blessings.

During Passover, Jesus would have sung Psalm 118 at the Last Supper, which was a Seder meal.

Retirement

Ask of me, and I will give the nations for your inheritance, the uttermost parts of the earth for your possession.

Psalm 2:8, WEB

Ask of me," God says, "and I will give you the world. You can possess all of it." The psalmist understands the great power and the great love behind those words: Ask of me. History taught the Israelites that those who defied God suffered, but those who obeyed God's decrees prospered. The psalmist must surely have wondered, "What can I ask of God that he will not grant?"

I'm putting money away for my retirement, but I'm not stressing out about how much I'll have or how much I'll need. When the time comes, I believe life will fall into place, and I'll know the direction I will want to take toward living differently or in a new place. I'm grateful, God, that I have my faith in You, for I believe that You will guide me toward the right decisions about my later years. I also believe that You have plans for me that will enrich my life. My job is to remember and follow Your advice on how to live and to trust that You will help me discover all that I need for a fulfilling retirement. I have only to ask.

Many Christians see Psalm 2 as a Messianic psalm that foretells of Jesus' coming.

Safety

For he shall give his angels charge over thee,
to keep thee in all thy ways.
They shall bear thee up in their hands,
lest thou dash thy foot against a stone.

Psalm 91:11–12, KJV

The Israelites knew God protected them in all ways. The psalmist tells us that God so cared for his children that he would bid his angels to lift them up above the stones on the roadways lest they bruise their feet. God spared no safeguards for his children.

God, thank You for helping me to remember and to feel Your ongoing protection. Whether I imagine myself a small child crawling into Your lap or I envision the comforting presence of angels, I know that I am blessed with heaven-sent armor against my earthbound fears. Sometimes those frights are simply nerves when I have to fly or drive on busy highways. Sometimes the terrors balloon into monsters I can't fight—the what-ifs of death, illness, or natural disasters. At those times, help me to remember to take a breath and relax into You, my guardian and my shield.

In Matthew 4:6, the Devil recites these verses from Psalm 91 as a way to tempt Jesus into obeying him.

Self-confidence

You prepare a table before me
in the presence of my enemies.
You anoint my head with oil;
my cup overflows.

Psalm 23:5, NIV

Among the Israelites, banquets offered opportunities for hosts to be generous. Guests dined on tempting delights and received the honor of having their heads perfumed with costly, scented oils. The guest who received an invitation to such a lavish affair considered himself fortunate.

Thank You, God, for inviting me into my own life, the life You generously gave me. Sometimes I've been too timid to open my mouth to say what I think or to ask for what I need. Sometimes I've been too frightened to try something new. I've definitely been too unsure of myself to say, "Let me do that. Give me a chance." Thanks for nudging this wallflower into taking a seat at the table. When I finally reached out to You, opened up my heart, and told You about my fears, You blessed me with confidence. I know You have faith in me, and Your sureness has made it possible for me to believe in myself.

In the psalmist's day, a host offered great honor to a guest by anointing his head with aromatic oils.

Setbacks

"Call on me in the day of trouble.
I will deliver you, and you will honor me."

Psalm 50:15, WEB

The singer speaks to his people with the conviction of a prophet, giving them God's words directly. His song reminds the faithful that God remembers the covenant God struck with the Israelites—obey my laws and I will make you a great nation. When you're in trouble, I will save you.

I was mad at You, because I wanted You to reverse a setback in my life, and it seemed like You were stalling me. I asked for a bailout, a redo, and all I heard was silence. I wondered how You could ignore one of Your children, so I stomped around and pouted. Hadn't Your covenant with me included Your promise to be there when I called? Back then, I hated Your silence, but today I'm grateful. When I stopped railing at You, at myself, and at life, I realized that my setback really was an opportunity that led me in a new and better direction. You hadn't been silent; You were prompting me to be patient. Only when I was at a standstill could I see that sometimes a setback is an unexpected gift, and I'm thankful for the one You gave to me.

Psalm 50 is one of the covenant renewal psalms, because it reminds the Israelites of their duties to God.

Sexuality

I will give thanks to you,
for I am fearfully and wonderfully made.
Your works are wonderful.
My soul knows that very well.

Psalm 139:14, WEB

The psalmist knows that God never takes his eyes off the child he has fashioned, for no part of the psalmist's body goes unnoticed by the creator. Since God fashioned him within the dark of his mother's womb, no moment of his life has been hidden from God. The psalmist takes comfort in knowing that he is always within God's sight and concern.

God, I know the psalmist declares me "wonderfully made," but I might quibble with some of my bits. I'd like a little less here, a little more there, maybe a different hair color, but that's the small stuff. I have nothing but thankfulness for this body that brings me such joy. Every second, my senses deliver gifts of sight and sound, touch, and taste. You also designed this body to give me the gift of pleasure; my sexuality makes me feel alive. The thrills from another's touch, the rising heat of my building desire, the moment of orgasm itself—Your gifts, to Your child, whose body works just as You intended.

➽ *USA Today* notes that both anti-abortion and gay-rights activists have used Verse 14 to support their positions.

Sleep

I have set the Lord always before me:
because he is at my right hand, I shall not be moved.
Therefore my heart is glad, and my glory rejoiceth:
my flesh also shall rest in hope.

Psalm 16:8–9, KJV

The psalmist, perhaps King David, delivers a song of confidence. God, he is certain, stands by him, ready to guide him and protect him. From that foundation of trust, the psalmist feels at ease. He is grateful that his mind, spirit, and body can take comfort from God and relax.

Sometimes I head for my bed, not because I'm sleepy but because I'm agitated. I want to hide, and what better way to calm my fears and restlessness than to burrow into my covers and disappear! God, I know that napping to avoid my anxieties is only a temporary tactic; it never works for long. Turning to You is a much better ploy for tackling life and staying awake. I'm grateful You stand near, ready to quiet my nerves and ease my troubles. With You at my side, my bedroom's no longer a hideout. Instead, I slip into my bed at night, push my cheek into my pillow, and pull the covers over my shoulders; I smile, sigh, and fall asleep because I'm secure in You.

St. Peter includes these verses in his first sermon (Acts 2:25–28), in which he discusses Jesus' resurrection.

Solitude

Behold, bless ye the Lord, all ye servants of the Lord,
which by night stand in the house of the Lord.
Lift up your hands in the sanctuary, and bless the Lord.

Psalm 134:1–2, KJV

When the Hebrews flocked to Jerusalem during their seasonal pilgrimages, the temple priests stood watch round the clock to serve and to pray with any of the faithful seeking a moment of quiet. Visible in the soft, flickering lights of the oil-burning menorah, the priests repeatedly lifted their arms in prayer. Sometimes they kept watch alone; but even in their solitude, they blessed the Lord.

Life's unexpected downtimes give me the blessing of solitude, and I relish the chance to be alone with my own thoughts. In those rare times when everyone but me is asleep, or when in the lingering twilight I watch the sun dip out of sight, my heart softens and opens more fully to life's mysteries. Like the solitary priests in the temple lifting their arms to God, I become fully present to You and my prayers for myself and others go heavenward. Like the priests, I too feel the holiness of solitude, for only in the stillness can I hear Your voice.

Psalm 134, the last of fifteen Psalms of Ascent sung on the temple pilgrimage, is a final song of praise.

Strangers

How excellent is Thy loving-kindness, O God!
therefore the children of men put their trust
under the shadow of thy wings.
They shall be abundantly satisfied with the fatness of thy house;

Psalm 36:7–8a, KJV

The psalmist knows he can rely on God's goodness and protection. It doesn't matter if evil lurks about, because God will protect and care for him. Like a nestling safe under its mother's outstretched wings, the psalmist knows he can trust in the abundance of God's nurturing love.

I'm grateful for the people who think "food" when they want to make someone feel welcome. When the world has seemed uncertain and foreign, a dinner invitation has always made me feel welcome. With knees tucked under the table and a fork tucked into warm food, who doesn't feel more like a friend and less like a stranger? Thank You for giving us families who set extra places for "orphans" at Thanksgiving or at the Seder meal, and for the smoky goodness of a backyard barbecue to greet a new neighbor, or the spread of nibbles at a baby shower to receive a tiny stranger whom no one has yet met. With hospitality, we can nurture each other, offering love and kindness to strangers, just as You hoped we would.

Verse 7 refers to the carvings of the cherubim, their wings protectively outstretched over the Ark of the Covenant.

Strength

Search me, O God, and know my heart:
try me, and know my thoughts:
And see if there be any wicked way in me,
and lead me in the way everlasting.

Psalm 139:23–24, KJV

Just as God is all-powerful and all knowing, the psalmist understands that God is everywhere, even in his very thoughts. How brave the psalmist is to invite God into his heart and mind and search them for any weaknesses. Only someone confident in God's love could be so brave.

God, it's so hard, sometimes impossible, to assess my strengths and weaknesses and then to give myself an assignment to do better. You, however, know me to my very core, which is why I'm thankful that You stand ready to help me ferret out the secrets of my heart and mind. God, I already know that You are the master of creation, so I trust You to give me a close examination and then lovingly participate in my re-creation. I'm not unhappy with the current "me"; in fact, I have some definite strengths. Still, a new and improved "me," guided by Your wisdom, sounds awesome. I'm thankful You're willing to roll up Your sleeves, dig into my heart and mind, and make me stronger.

Since around the fourth century, psalms have been part of monastic daily prayer.

Terrorism

Why do the nations rage,
and the peoples plot a vain thing?

Psalm 2:1, WEB

The ancient scribes who organized the Book of Psalms chose this one to be among the opening songs. The poet urges the Israelites to remember that individuals are not the only ones who are called to embrace good and reject evil. Nations also have a relationship with God; and those that reject godliness, God will reject and punish.

Today, somewhere in this world, people are plotting against others. Perhaps they wish to terrorize someone of a different faith, a different gender, or a different ethnicity. Maybe they want to crush their political enemies. Possibly they simply are driven by hatred or led by zealots who believe that revenge equals righteousness. Regardless of their motives, they cause suffering and create fear. God, I am not thankful for those who destroy peace between peoples, but I am thankful for You, because I believe You will call these fanatics to account for their crimes. You will remind them that a just God rules, not terrorists pretending to be gods.

In the Book of Acts (4:24–26), St. Paul notes King David as the author of Psalm 2.

Theft

The Lord protects the unwary;
when I was brought low, he saved me.
Return to your rest, my soul,
for the Lord has been good to you.

Psalm 116:6–7, NIV

The psalmist clearly is coming back from hard times. Like someone who has faced death, or severe illness, or a personal setback, he is relieved to have survived his time of trial. Nevertheless, he hasn't forgotten his moments of fear or pain, or the times when he prayed to God for rescue. Now safe and secure, he reassures himself that he can relax, because God has been good to him and protected him from harm.

Headlines about identity theft and hackers trolling for credit card and social security numbers make me nervous. What if some thief hacks my financial data? I'm afraid I'll discover that my VISA has made a luxury vacation possible for some unscrupulous stranger, while I hunker down at home and try to undo the damage. Then thankfully I remember that You'll see me through whatever happens. No, You won't catch the thief and You won't talk to my bank, but You will talk to me. You'll remind me that keeping in touch with You will keep me steady even should villains cross my path.

Martin Luther said Psalm 116 belonged to the First Commandment, because it honors God and calls upon his name.

Time

My times are in your hand.
Deliver me from the hand of my enemies,
and from those who persecute me.

Psalm 31:15, WEB

The Book of Daniel recounts the story of a young Hebrew noble taken captive into Babylon. Through several dreams, God gives Daniel the wisdom to know that God controls changes through time and even the rise and fall of kings (Dn 2:21). God sets and winds the human timepiece.

God, Your hand synchronizes the rhythms of life. The seasons arrive unassisted. In the sky, birds heed Your plan and hurry to gather nesting materials or lift their wings in mass migration. The crocus pops out its purple head, the wheat turns to gold, the orchards hang with fruit, and the bear lumbers to its winter cave and snugs in. All is in Your hands, including me. I'm grateful for Your help in prevailing over those things that vacuum up my time—social media time, work time, television time, and gaming time. Thanks for helping me to embrace friend time, family time, and You-and-me time. Your wisdom helps to guide me toward the hours that count the most as I try to build a life filled with quality time.

The word "times," or "eth" in Hebrew, can mean the passage of time, but also a person's fortunes.

Violence

We have sinned with our fathers,
we have committed iniquity,
we have done wickedly.

Psalm 106:6, KJV

The psalmist knows that the Israelites were never without sin. From the time of Moses and the Exodus to their exile in Babylonia, the Israelites often displeased God. Therefore, the poet writes a psalm that honestly recounts his peoples' transgressions. In admitting to a nation's sins, the psalmist hopes to garner God's mercy and blessing.

Like the sinful Israelites who ignored Your commandments, the people in my nation have not always done their best. God, when You said, "Love your neighbor," my ancestors engaged in the violence of selling slaves or forcing children into sweatshops instead of schools. When You told us to care for one another as You have cared for us, we left homeless veterans, the mentally ill, or the poor to wander our streets and endure harsh indignities. When You asked us to deal honestly with each other, we let our greed collapse our banks and foreclose on people's homes. Thankfully, God, You do not hold these lapses against us. You forgive; You remind us; and when we forget, thankfully You try again.

This psalm is often paired with Psalm 105, which also is a history psalm, but with a more joyous tone.

War

The earth is the Lord's, and everything in it,
the world, and all who live in it;
for he founded it on the seas
and established it on the waters.

Psalm 24:1–2, NIV

The Israelites took comfort in knowing that all of creation belonged to God, for it was God who fashioned the land and enlivened it with every variety of life. God also chose to share his creation with his chosen ones, and they sang their grateful praise.

I cannot silence the guns that boom in warfare. I cannot still the tanks, ground the planes, or send the soldiers home. We humans have fought each other for thousands of years. We have killed each other in obedience to kings, emperors, and elected leaders who no longer command armies. I am not grateful for war, God. It pains me that Your children squabble, sometimes even to the death over lands and resources that were never theirs to begin with. I give thanks when I remember that these lands, their citizens, and their possessions belong to You, and I trust You to protect all that You possess and love. That knowledge, dear God, takes me past my war-torn sorrows and into a hopefulness that You can see a world more peaceful than today's.

Psalm 24 carries listeners back to Genesis and God's creation story.

Don't be like the horse, or like the mule,
which have no understanding,
who are controlled by bit and bridle,
or else they will not come near to you.

Psalm 32:9, WEB

In his penitential poem, the psalmist sings of the relief that comes from knowing that God forgives sinners and that it feels good to confess transgressions. He encourages the faithful to behave like right-thinking people and not like stubborn animals. Come near your God; hear his voice. Don't mimic the beasts that must be tethered and pulled in the right direction.

God, at first my pride kept me from understanding Your "Help Wanted" notice. I was looking for grand and important work, but You were looking for someone to sit at a bedside. I wanted to save the world and garner recognition for my great deeds, but You needed a tutor in the after-school program. I wanted to lend my strong voice to a great cause, and You sought another voice in the choir. Thankfully, I turned my pride off and my hearing on. When I listened to You and realized all the work that needs to be done, I went from wanting to feel important to seeking the challenge of doing important work for You.

Psalm 32, an atonement prayer in the early church, is still recited on Yom Kippur, the Jewish Day of Atonement.

Worry

The Lord is my light and my salvation;
whom shall I fear?
the Lord is the strength of my life;
of whom shall I be afraid?

Psalm 27:1, KJV

The psalmist is both worried and confident. Perhaps he sees his enemy in the distance, yet he feels certain that he has nothing to fear. Perhaps his enemy's strength or cleverness makes him feel momentarily vulnerable, but he remains steadfast. He's not worried, because God is on his side.

I'm grateful that when I reach out to You, I can feel Your warmth and strength seep into my spirit and subdue my worries, no matter how small or random. With You, I'm not a nameless nobody; rather I'm a troubled child seeking comfort; and as my parent, You do not fail me. When anxieties and fears darken my thoughts, You are my light. When I feel doomed to failure or find myself too fearful to embrace a challenge, You are my salvation. I have learned that as a child of God, I can bring my apprehensions to You and You will exchange them for a blessed assurance that You stand near me.

With its "light" and "salvation," this verse is seen as having a strong connection to the Jewish Day of Atonement.

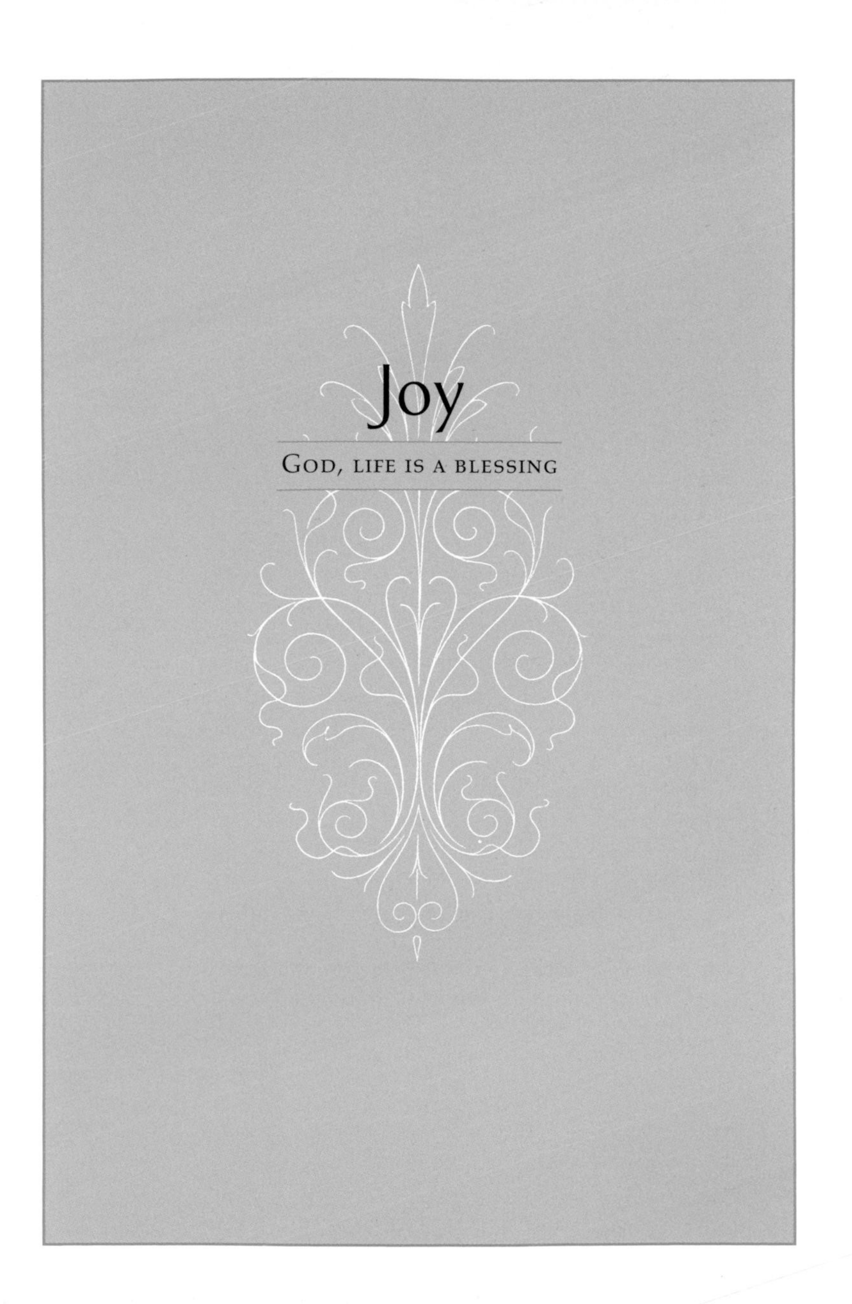

Joy

God, life is a blessing

Aging

Planted in the house of the Lord,
They will flourish in the courts of our God.
They will still yield fruit in old age;
They shall be full of sap and very green,

Psalm 92:13–14, NASB

The Israelites found the upside of aging, for in old age they enjoyed the wisdom that comes from experience and patience. The palm and fig trees growing in their homes' central courtyards yielded shade and fruit, even as the trees aged. As observant people of God's plan, they knew that even when old, they were still full of sap—full of vigor and usefulness.

God, I love these verses; they have no downside. The words make me smile, because they remind me that even as my wrinkles come, my joints stiffen, and my parts get saggy, it's no big deal. You have given me the promise of a resilient and energetic spirit. You have told me that even as my body changes, my wisdom will grow, and I will be useful to You and to those who love me. Help me to hold on to this joy and the self-assurance that comes with knowing that old age is not a curse, but a destination, and You are traveling with me.

Psalm 92, with the title "Song for the Sabbath Day," is recited in the synagogue on Saturday, the Jewish Sabbath.

Death

Surely your goodness and love will follow me
all the days of my life,
and I will dwell in the house of the Lord
forever.

Psalm 23:6, NIV

The Psalmist, possibly King David himself, sings from a deep, unshakeable faith. God's love will be as close as the air he breathes, and God's invitation into the house of the Lord is true and unconditional.

The moment of my death is a secret known only to You, God. Someday I will step into that mystery. Yes, it scares me at times to think about dying. I confess that I struggle to imagine this world without me in it, but then I stop myself. Why imagine this world without me, when I can turn my imagination toward life forever with You? I know Your goodness and love has followed me everywhere, and Your presence brings me joy. How much greater will my joy be when I step across Your welcome mat and enter the home You have prepared for me?

A Native American version ends, "I will go to live in the Big Teepee and sit down with the Shepherd Chief forever."

Decisions

But I have trusted in thy mercy;
my heart shall rejoice in thy salvation.
I will sing unto the Lord,
because he hath dealt bountifully with me.

Psalm 13:5–6, KJV

In spite of enemies that brought him low, the psalmist proclaims a joyful truth; he trusts God to deliver him, not only from his enemies, but also from himself. Yes, he has experienced hard times; and in those moments, he sometimes feared that the Lord had left his side: perhaps forever. His panic, however, was only momentary, and the psalmist sings praises to God, whose love is steadfast.

What a relief, God, to look back on the decisions I've made and to see them more clearly. Which college? Which internship? Which invitation? Life was about choices, and they all seemed monumental. I made some in haste and some without wisdom. Too often, I made them without You; I didn't trust You to guide me to life's fun and adventure. Life still throws decisions my way, but with Your help, I am better at sorting them into piles: "Important" and "Trivial." Then we sit down together to think the "Important" ones through, and with You next to me, I have the confidence to make wise decisions.

The Book of Psalms includes several individual laments that share a common theme: Distress dissolves when one remembers God.

Depression

That you may give him rest from the days of adversity,
until the pit is dug for the wicked.
For Yahweh won't reject his people,
neither will he forsake his inheritance.

Psalm 94:13–14, WEB

The Israelites knew trouble, and then they found rest, for the enemies that plagued them dropped away as if their evilness had pushed them into a deep hole. The psalmist joyfully recalls that God does not turn away from his people. Perhaps he remembered the words of the prophet Isaiah, "I will make darkness light before them, and crooked things straight. These things will I do unto them, and not forsake them." (Is 42:16, KJV)

People aren't the only ones pressed down and in a slump, God. We're struggling with a depressed economy and housing market. We're glum about unemployment rates that could go even higher and investment returns that could drop even lower. Economic pressures take an emotional toll on us all. Nevertheless, when I hear "economic depression," I refuse to get gloomy, because I know You bring the light to any darkness whether that is my humble budget or the larger world's economic woes. I know that when I include You in my fortunes, I too rest from the blues.

This psalm inspired Julius Reubke's "Sonata on the 94th Psalm in C minor," a composition well known among organists.

Disappointment

Lord my God, You have done many things—
Your wonderful works and Your plans for us;
none can compare with You.
If I were to report and speak of them,
they are more than can be told.

Psalm 40:5, HCSB

The psalmist starts his poem with the story of a man spiritually mired down. He feels like he has slogged through a swamp or has been abandoned in a pit of self-destruction. Perhaps it is King David lamenting; but whoever is in trouble, he calls out to God. He has confidence that God's plan for him will include his deliverance, for such is the greatness of God.

God, I finally am able to believe in this truth: You never disappoint. I admit, I've been a slow learner. Sometimes I got impatient when I thought You weren't answering my prayers, and sometimes I felt ignored. Then I finally came to see that Your plans for me were always better than what I had asked for; I just had to be patient until You showed me what I really needed. I know I'll continue to face life's disappointments, but coming to trust that You'll never let me down is now a source of joy.

Methodist pastor Henry J. Zelley wrote the Gospel hymn "He Brought Me Out," which comes directly from Psalm 40.

Distractions

Praise ye him, sun and moon: praise him, all ye stars of light.
Fire, and hail; snow, and vapour; stormy wind fulfilling his word:
Mountains, and all hills; fruitful trees, and all cedars:
Beasts, and all cattle; creeping things, and flying fowl:

Psalm 148:3, 8-10, KJV

The psalmist urges not only the Israelites, but also the entire world to witness God's glorious creation and to sing praises to the creator. He calls upon the heavenly bodies to praise God night and day with their bright lights. From heat to ice, from the tallest mountains to the humblest of hills, from the wild animals to the tame, everything on Earth offers its "hallelujah" to God, the master of creation.

God, You are the master of creation and a master at distraction, for You tempt my eyes, my ears, my taste buds, and my nose with life's delights. When I'm bogged down with work, bird chirps and blue skies distract me with an invitation to take a stroll. When my heart is heavy with worries, You tune up the volume on laughter, music, or a cat's soothing purr. I can't deny that life is stressful, but when I let Your creation distract me with its beauty, my life revels in moments of joy.

Psalm 148 forms the core of the Benedicite, or "Song of Creation," sung by Lutherans, Catholics, and Anglicans during worship.

Dreams

How precious also are thy thoughts unto me, O God!
how great is the sum of them!
If I should count them, they are more in number than the sand:
when I awake, I am still with thee.

Psalm 139:17–18, KJV

In this psalm, the poet affirms his deep trust in an all-knowing and all-powerful God. In these verses, however, the poet focuses on the immensity of God's thoughts, which are more numerous than grains of sand on the beach and which contain all the wisdom of the universe. The poet finds comfort in knowing that some of God's great and wise thoughts turn toward the poet. How comforting to be among God's thoughts.

I've heard that our dreams contain our most private fears and hopes. Deep in slumber, we process through our days—what we felt and what we did—in ways that even we don't understand. Our dreams are windows into ourselves, into the deepest recesses of our hearts and minds. I happily invite You into my dreams, to excavate deep into my being and to help me unravel the mysteries of me. My omnipresent God, be with me as I sleep and let Your wisdom fuse with my reveries, so that even in my dreams, I am with You.

Many scholars consider Psalm 139 to be among the greatest in the Psalter.

Environment

The earth is the Lord's, and all it contains,
The world, and those who dwell in it.
For He has founded it upon the seas
And established it upon the rivers.

Psalm 24:1–2, NASB

When the Ark of the Covenant entered the temple in Jerusalem, worshipers broke out in song. Everything on this earth belongs to God, the psalmist intoned, and he is present everywhere not just in this temple, not just with those tablets of stone.

Where am I God? Where does Your world end and where does mine begin? I'm joyful, because I know the answers. I live in Your world, and everything in Your world, including me, belongs to You. This news makes me smile, because it makes things simple, yet sound. Your world doesn't end at my front door, it includes my very home. The couch and the people who nap on it? All Yours. The beds where we dream, make love, and snore are Yours, as well as those dreamers and lovers and noisemakers. If You claim every inch of our environment, then every inch is holy ground and every person blessed. What joyful news!

Roman Catholics often hear Psalm 24 read at the funerals of children.

Faith

I will sing of the loving kindness of Yahweh forever.
With my mouth, I will make known your faithfulness to all generations.
I indeed declare, "Love stands firm forever.
You established the heavens.
Your faithfulness is in them."

Psalm 89:1–2, WEB

The psalmist sings with gratefulness and deep faith as he recounts the prophecy the oracle Nathan gave to David (2 Sm 7:8–16). God will not leave David's side; he will protect him and destroy his enemies. David shall rule over the Israelites, and they will have a resting place safe from their foes. From David will come an heir who will establish a great kingdom, and the House of David and this kingdom will remain secure forever.

Nothing in this world is permanent, except for You, my God. Your voice from ancient times summons me to open my heart and my life to You; in return, You have promised me Your steadfast love and protection. That the creator of the universes should bend my way, stand next to me, and wait for my attention fills me with awe. Oh, God of the desert peoples, You gave King David confidence and hope, just as Your promise of a never-ending love now nurtures joy in my heart.

Jews hold Psalm 89 dear because it offers the enduring statement of God's faithfulness to the Hebrews.

Family

The Lord is merciful and gracious,
slow to anger, and plenteous in mercy.
He will not always chide:
neither will he keep his anger for ever.

Psalm 103:8–9, KJV

In this most joyful of songs, the psalmist sings praises to God for his ongoing love and support. Like a good parent, God lays down the law, but is quick to forgive any of his children who do not always follow the rules.

My family brings me happiness, God, and because of You, I wholeheartedly nurture them with joy. Through Your example of enduring love and generous forgiveness, You've shown me how to be a good parent and a loving spouse. Families aren't always easy, as You well know. Those Israelites tried Your patience; but even when they disobeyed, You never turned away. You stood by them until they came to their senses. Like You, I let my kids know that I may not like their naughtiness, but I'll always love them. With You as my teacher on how to create a faithful and loving household, my family and I will know joy in You and in each other. We praise You, Lord.

In this psalm of joyful praise, the psalmist cries out six times, "Praise the Lord!"

Friends

Look on my right, and see;
for there is no one who is concerned for me.
Refuge has fled from me.
No one cares for my soul.

Psalm 142:4, WEB

For an Israelite, the person standing at his right hand was the person he trusted to have his back. The psalmist looks to his right and finds no one willing to stand by him, no one willing to fight with him or for him. He stands alone and laments that no one cares whether he lives or dies.

I know it's in vogue to christen someone a "BFF"—Best Friend Forever. So, I'm not trying to be hip when I say that I have more than one BFF. Unlike the psalmist who finds himself alone and without anyone to call "friend," I look around and see many smiling faces, and I feel many supportive hands. God, You have blessed me with close companions. I can turn to them and cry, "Help," and they'll come running. I can turn a sad eye their way, and they'll give me their shoulder to cry on. They stand not only to my right, but also to my left, and even behind me, so I know the joy of journeying through life with others.

Psalm 142 may recount when David, fearing for his life, hid in a cave to elude King Saul.

Happiness

You have turned my mourning into dancing for me.
You have removed my sackcloth,
and clothed me with gladness,
To the end that my heart may sing praise to you,
and not be silent.

Psalm 30:11–12a, WEB

When the Israelites were in trouble, they wore sackcloth and ashes. Even the king exchanged his fine garments for the clothing of woe. God saw their sadness and sent them joy, and their hearts danced.

God, thanks to You my life now moves to a happier beat, and I'm dancing with joy. I've had some times where I moved through my life as if I had two left feet, tripping over myself and everyone else. Now I feel like I'm line dancing with the best of them, moving in easy rhythm with You and the people around me. I wake up eager to get going. I look forward to digging into the day's work and using my brain and my body to get the jobs done. I laugh more than I cry; I smile more than I frown. I give more than I take, and I love fully. Look at me, God, I'm twisting and shouting for joy!

Sackcloth is a coarse, rough fabric woven from camel or goat hair or from plant fibers like hemp.

Health

My friends and companions avoid me
because of my wounds;
my neighbors stay far away.

Psalm 38:11, NIV

The Israelites often abandoned the ailing, for surely this person with open sores or delirium must have committed some offense before God. Afflicted with boils, Job found himself alone, forsaken by friends and rebuked by others. Loneliness and rejection clung to the infirm.

God, You tucked a gift into my illness. I may be sick, but I come before You with joy, because in this time of pain and worry, You have brought me the offering of love. Unlike Job or the forsaken psalmist, I have been enfolded by my family and friends' tender concern. My hospital room has been filled with the laughter and encouragement of those who keep me company. My kitchen overflows with homemade meals. I don't know when or if I'll get better, for my journey to recovery is not easy; but daily You reassure me that I will not be left alone to fret and fuss. I may be ailing, but within the certainty of sickness comes the unexpected joy of being loved.

Biblical scholars generally agree that most of the psalms were written for communal worship in the temple.

Home

How lovely is your dwelling place,
Lord Almighty!
My soul yearns, even faints,
for the courts of the Lord;
my heart and my flesh cry out
for the living God.

Psalm 84:1–2, NIV

For the Hebrews, the temple was their spiritual home and the central core of their lives. Extended families joyously made annual pilgrimages to the temple and eagerly anticipated traveling together to worship in the majesty of the Lord's house.

Thinking about my home fills me with joy. Even when I'm away, I can picture its cozy corners, feel the couch cushions against my legs, and smell the aroma of morning coffee or dinner in the oven. I hear the voices of loved ones and imagine them in their places—easy chair, kitchen table, study desk, patio. Sometimes I ache just to be there, for I have woven my life into this temple, which You have helped me fashion out of love and hard work. When I stand within this sanctuary, I know that I am blessed and that You are with me within its walls.

Psalm 84 is among the psalms known as the "Pilgrim Psalms," for it speaks to the longing for God's temple.

Loneliness

I love the Lord, because He hears
My voice and my supplications.
Because He has inclined His ear to me,
Therefore I shall call upon Him as long as I live.

Psalm 116:1–2, NASB

The psalmist dives into his song with an immediate declaration of his love for God. When the poet struggled, God listened to him and heard his pleas for help. With God at his side, the psalmist knows he can face anything, because he is secure in God's love.

I've known too many moments when I've felt adrift and by myself. I can't count the times when I've sat stiff and conspicuous at a table for one, and I've gone solo to too many movies and museums. Then there were those days when the house felt too big for just me, and my contentment seemed to shrivel with the knowledge that I was alone. Yet even in those times, God, I could still say with confidence, "I love the Lord," and those words rescued me from loneliness. While I slip occasionally into woe-is-me solitary spells, I know that as long as You love me, I am never truly alone, and that truth will always be a source of joy.

Psalm 116 is a deeply personal prayer, for depending on the translation, almost every verse includes a first-person pronoun.

Money

Yahweh assigned my portion and my cup.
You made my lot secure.
The lines have fallen to me in pleasant places.
Yes, I have a good inheritance.

Psalm 16:5–6, WEB

The psalmist may be recalling David's story from when King Saul hunted David and chased him from his homeland and his inheritance. Though in danger, David lifted his fears to God and placed his confidence in the one who offered an eternal inheritance. In the time of Moses, God told Aaron, "I am your portion and your inheritance among the children of Israel" (Nm 18:20, WEB). David would have known these words and would have placed great trust in their promise.

God, I may not inherit much money, but I have already received a rich legacy. I have the security of family bonds. My parents invested their lives in me and deposited deep within me guidance on how to live a fruitful life. Their love and support helped me know that I am a credit to them. My friends also have invested in me, and their listening ears, their laughter, and their concern have paid enormous dividends. I'm prosperous in the ways that matter, and then there's my inheritance from You—wealth I can take to the bank for eternity.

In Hebrew times, an inheritance divided among sons involved the casting of lots and God's involvement in the apportioning.

Nature

Make a joyful noise to Yahweh, all the earth!
Burst out and sing for joy, yes, sing praises!
Let the sea roar with its fullness;
the world, and those who dwell therein.
Let the rivers clap their hands.
Let the mountains sing for joy together.

Psalm 98:4, 7–8, WEB

The Israelites gathered in the temple among the assembled musicians and joyously honored God with triumphant music. With harp and timbrel, lyre and drum and full voices, they offered up jubilant sounds to show their joy not only in God's creation, but also in his faithfulness to them.

Just as composers have created lofty orchestral works to honor kings and emperors, so Your kingdom, God, honors You with a symphony of sound—cymbal-crashing thunder, drum beats of raindrops, horn blasts of wind, and castanets of river waters dashing over rocks. Our orchestral works and musicians showcase glorious, heart-stopping music, but even these are lesser versions of the noisemakers You created and placed on nature's stage. Help me to feel through nature's music the joy of Your presence in my life, for You are as near as the rustle of leaves, the crack of lightning, and the tender coo of the morning dove.

Psalm 98 is considered one of the "royal" psalms, because its noble language suggests nature bowing before its king.

Neighbor

He heals the broken in heart,
and binds up their wounds.
He counts the number of the stars.
He calls them all by their names.

Psalm 147:3–4, WEB

With years of heartache behind them, the Hebrews returned from exile to their beloved Jerusalem. They joyfully chanted this hymn of praise to God. The poet's words reminded them of Isaiah's, declaring that God called forth the stars by name (Is 40:26). If God can hold the stars close to his heart, how much more so the people he loves?

The Milky Way with its billons of stars appears like a smear of light in the night sky, yet You know every star by name. The earth carries more than seven billion people, and while I can call only a few by name, You know us all. Your stars have much to teach me about neighbors. It doesn't matter if I can name them, I have only to remember that we link our lives through You, our shared creator. When the world seems filled with strangers, I have only to look to the heavens to be reminded that my neighbors live in every corner of Your creation, and with joy and love, You call each of us by name.

Scholars date this psalm to the fifth century BCE, after the return from exile and the rebuilding of Jerusalem's temple.

Networking

May the Lord silence all flattering lips
and every boastful tongue—
those who say, "By our tongues we will prevail;
our own lips will defend us—who is lord over us?"

Psalm 12:3–4, NIV

The psalmist bemoans smooth talkers who spew falsehoods instead of the truth. Their mouths open and feigned flattery pops out. So bold are they in their lies that they foolishly believe that their words will win arguments and that their dishonest voices will even prevail over God's. The poet, however, is not fooled, for he and God know they have false hearts.

I hear too many falsehoods—in the news, in campaign speeches, and certainly in the barrage of ads trying to sell me stuff. Sometimes I feel assaulted by this network of false communicators. Most often, however, I joyfully remember that I belong to a different network, a network of well-meaning people whose voices reflect respect and regard for others. I hear this network of voices at church, at work, in social groups, and in my family. I trust the people in these networks, for their words are not weapons and they are not bent on deceit. These voices make me smile, because they remind me that Your voice has sway in the human network.

The ancient Hebrew language did not use vowels, so how the psalms sounded when sung remains a mystery.

Noise

O sing unto the Lord a new song,
for he hath done marvellous things:
his right hand, and his holy arm,
hath gotten him the victory.

Psalm 98:1, KJV

God kept his promise to the Israelites and numbered their descendants beyond the tally of the stars in heaven. In joyfulness, they put a new song into their hymnals and sang out their praise.

Today I promise to live my life as a new song with lyrics that are open to the human experience and worthy of Your gifts to me. Instead of being out of tune, I'll jazz up life's humdrum with deep laughter. May my prayers have the soulfulness of ballads and my blues notes the honesty of self-awareness and not blame. Forgive me if I occasionally croon off key, and I'll remind myself to sing new melodies in harmony with others. When I'm worried or sad, may I waltz slowly with You, Your hand gently pressed against my back guiding me to new tempos of hope and resilience. Help me to feel life's steady rhythm coming at me through joyful noise and help me to contribute to the happy sound with my own new songs.

Some Bible scholars wonder if Mary of Nazareth sang Psalm 98, for her own "Magnificat" follows the psalmist's sentiments.

People

Blessed is the nation whose God is Yahweh,
the people whom he has chosen for his own inheritance.
Yahweh looks from heaven.
He sees all the sons of men.

Psalm 33:12–13, WEB

In this hymn of praise, the poet reminds the faithful that God keeps a watchful eye on people everywhere, not just those living in the Promised Land. However, God has chosen the Israelites as his special ones. He will make of them a great nation even as he bestows upon them his eternal inheritance.

Though we number in the billions, You see each of us, and You see into all of us. I want to see these multitudes as You do, with an open and accepting love. What comfort to know that each of us is special to You and that Your love brushes aside skin color and varying physical and mental abilities. You pay no attention to gender, sexual orientation, and general human quirkiness. Because You made us, You embrace all that we are and guide us to all that we can be. Just as You see all of us, You ask us to see all of You in everyone we meet. You challenge us, God, even as You push us toward loving all Your people.

It is likely Psalm 33 was written as a hymn and possibly one meant to be performed with a chorus.

Popularity

The stone the builders rejected
has become the cornerstone;
the Lord has done this,
and it is marvelous in our eyes.

Psalm 118:22–23, NIV

The poet understands that a sound building happens when the mason carefully chooses each stone. For the cornerstone, however, he's even more particular, because that stone sets the strength and position of the entire structure. The Israelites often felt rejected by others, but the psalmist reminds them that they are the cornerstones upon which God chose to build a great nation.

Rejection is hard to accept, and I've been on the hurtful side of rebuffs. Today, however, I live with the confidence that You have chosen me. I can bypass the I-want-to-be-popular trap, because You've helped me to build something more secure—my faith in You and in the loving people You have placed in my life and with whom I'm building something enduring. Rejection hurts, but real life isn't a popularity contest. The true contest starts with two questions: "Do I like myself?" and "Does God like me?" When the answer is "yes" to both, then I can tear up the popularity ballots and know that I'm a chosen child of God who flourishes on a strong foundation.

➛ **The First Epistle of Peter (2:4) links the rejected stone to Jesus, who was rejected as the Messiah.**

Poverty

The Lord is my shepherd;
I shall not want.

Psalm 23:1, KJV

This psalm speaks an observable truth; sheep follow their shepherd. To the Israelites, an equally deep truth was that God, like a diligent, untiring shepherd, cared for his flock. When in their shepherd's care, the Israelites lacked for nothing.

Hallelujah! I have everything I need, God, including the wisdom You've given me to know the difference between what I yearn for and what's vital to my life. I appreciate my essential gifts—love, family, a roof above and food in the cupboard, a job, and friends to laugh with and lean on. Oh, I have my days when I crave more, when I complain that I'm tired of being poor, or when I worry that this month's paycheck won't cover everything. That's just my short-term whining, God, because You have made me rich. I can smile and say, "Poverty, get away from my door, because this lamb has the greatest of shepherds."

Many say Psalm 23 foreshadows Jesus, who is often pictured as a shepherd with his lambs.

Relationships

Satisfy us in the morning with your unfailing love,
that we may sing for joy and be glad all our days.

Psalm 90:14, NIV

The psalmist sings a lament for the community—life is short, life is hard, and for mere mortals life is filled with limitations. God, however, is omnipotent and everlasting. The psalmist reminds the prayerful that God has formed a covenant with them, and God's steadfast love will bring the Israelites not only security, but also joy.

God, our relationship is solid. You're my confidant, my counselor, and my coach, but You're also my source of comfort. Everyone needs a best friend to turn to when life gets tough, and I've learned that sometimes relationships are part of life's rough spots. So, when my relationships become a struggle or feel out of balance, I have You as my go-to guy. When I problem-solve with You, I get a better sense of when I need to try harder with someone or when I need to let a relationship find its own way. You've taught me that building bonds with others takes effort, but that relationships shouldn't be all work. They should also grow joy. I know I have to keep working at my relationship with You, but when I do, I reap the benefits of a contented spirit.

Psalm 90 focuses on *chesed*, the Hebrew word for God's unfailing love, which steadfastly binds God to the Israelites.

Retirement

I will dwell in your tent forever.
I will take refuge in the shelter of your wings. Selah.
For you, God, have heard my vows.
You have given me the heritage of those who fear your name.

Psalm 61:4–5, WEB

The poet thinks longingly of God's holy temple, a place of refuge and comfort. He knows that as God's child, he can rely on his father to protect him and to provide an inheritance. For the psalmist, this birthright does not come as costly gold or livestock, but as the limitless treasure to live forever in God's favor.

I don't know what retirement will be like or how much it will cost. Investment advisors show me numbers, but they don't know how long I'll live or if I'll be healthy. I don't know what role an IRA, a 401K, or a Keogh Plan plays or if those savings will carry me through all the years I hope to live. Who can know? I know retirement is approaching, but it barrels my way with no assured strategy. So, God, I'm grateful that one thing is guaranteed in my investment portfolio: You. I am Your child, and You have secured my inheritance, and such a legacy enriches my earthly retirement.

Some scholars suggest David wrote Psalm 61 when he feared King Saul or his own son Absalom would harm him.

Safety

The Lord is with me; I will not be afraid.
What can mere mortals do to me?
The Lord is with me; he is my helper.
I look in triumph on my enemies.

Psalm 118:6–7, NIV

The psalmist appears to be praying for himself, but it is clear in the full psalm that his song of thanksgiving is lifted on behalf of a nation. As in other poems, the psalmist declares with confidence that when God is on the Israelites' side, no enemy can prevail against them nor can fears defeat them.

My mind and heart are at peace, because I feel safe—in my home, in my neighborhood, with others, and with myself. Given news reports and troubling headlines, I know it's not easy to feel secure in this world, but I have come to believe that You are with me, God. When I fall into my bed at night, I feel blessed, because life feels steady and I do not know fear. My well-being doesn't grow from naiveté, because I know troubling things happen in this world. My sense of security comes from You, from knowing that even if something or someone unsettles me, I can lean into You, my no-fail safety net.

Psalm 118 was Martin Luther's favorite: "...this psalm proved a friend and helped me out of many great troubles."

Self-confidence

I am still confident of this:
I will see the goodness of Yahweh in the land of the living.

Psalm 27:13, WEB

Throughout Psalm 27, the psalmist asserts his deep, unwavering belief in God. His song sings of the good times, and it sings of the bad. Yet, through the unpredictable nature of life, the singer keeps a true north with God. He stands steadfast with Yahweh, even as he is confident that Yahweh stands steadfast with him.

Through the years, I've learned how to project self-confidence—dress for success, stand tall, give a firm handshake, and look people in the eye. That confident style works in a job interview, and maybe even that first meeting with future in-laws, but You've guided me toward a different plan for building my self-confidence. First, I'll trust in You. Second, I'll try to be more like You in this world. I'll get a confident voice by speaking up for others. I'll feel confident that my life is good by remembering to be grateful for all You've given me. I'll know I matter when the people I've helped say "Thanks," or "I couldn't have done this without you." It's in living rightly with others that I'll polish my self-confidence and that I'll see You in their faces smiling back at me.

Christians read this verse at funeral services, having interpreted it to mean that those who die live with God.

Setbacks

Yet he took note of their distress
when he heard their cry;
for their sake he remembered his covenant
and out of his great love he relented.

Psalm 106:44–45, NIV

In a long string of shameful reminders, the psalmist harkens back to the days when the Israelites tested God's patience and rebelled against God's law. In spite of God's goodness and Moses' struggles to deliver them to the Promised Land, they worshipped false gods and grumbled against God and Moses. Though they had been faithless and disobedient, God remembered his promise to care for them, and God's heart softened.

I'm embarrassed when I recall that I've made some dreadful decisions and some compromising choices. Looking back, I'm not surprised that I suffered such setbacks. I made gods out of the wrong people and worshipped shaky goals. When things didn't go my way, I blamed others and couldn't see that many of my setbacks came more from my own shortsightedness. I strayed from You, but fortunately, You did not wander away from me. You reached into my head and heart, and reminded me that faithfulness to my values would be the key to my success.

The Psalter includes five books, and Psalm 106 is the closing song in the fourth Book of Psalms.

Sexuality

All the paths of the Lord
are lovingkindness and truth
to those who keep His covenant
and His testimonies.

Psalm 25:10, NASB

The poet travels a path of remembrance, singing a psalm to remind the Hebrews of their ancestors' grave sin when they fashioned and worshipped a golden calf, even as Moses accepted God's laws on Mount Sinai. In their weakness, they had sought the comfort of an idol that brought instant gratification. They had been unfaithful to their God, who nevertheless offered them his unwavering devotion and forgiveness.

I've learned that it's not enough to feel or look sexy. Buff bodies, burning desire, and being on the prowl for a partner may all carry quick excitement, but they do not bring a joy that grows from knowing you are loved and treasured, even with wrinkles, a paunch, or thinning hair. You meant for Your gift of sexuality to bring Your children comfort and connection, but You also expected us to bring the glue of loving faithfulness to our most intimate moments. You taught us how to use our sexuality responsibly, and our joy comes from the security and contentment of knowing another loves us fully.

Psalm 25 includes the Hebrew word *chesed*, which translates to "loving-kindness," or the special relationship God has with his beloved.

Sleep

It is vain for you to rise up early,
to stay up late, eating the bread of toil;
for he gives sleep to his loved ones.

Psalm 127:2, WEB

The Israelites physically labored to make their pilgrimages to the temple. Their muscles ached and their heads grew sweaty. Along the way, they often had to defend themselves against wild animals or unsavory characters. Their journey was not easy, and they did not worship the work of getting to the temple; they treasured the destination, which brought both physical and spiritual rest.

Hallelujah, God. You understand downtime, for even You rested after the six-day job of creation. I know workaholics, the people who see time at their desks as more valuable than time at the dinner table, and that's not me. I don't feel guilty when I put my feet up at the end of the day, or get a board game to play with others, or when I steal away for a quick nap. I have You to thank for reminding me that hard work is good and necessary, but moments of refreshment also are essential to good work and a good life. So, when it's time for bed, I'm ready to enjoy Your gift of a secure and restful sleep.

Many who comment on the psalms see Psalm 127 as a recommended poem for workaholics.

Solitude

God, you are my God.
I will earnestly seek you.
My soul thirsts for you.
My flesh longs for you, in a dry and weary land,
where there is no water.

Psalm 63:1, WEB

The poet starts, "A psalm of David, when he was in the wilderness of Judah." The prayerful certainly can recall the troubled king, chased by enemies and living just on the edges of society in the scrubby pastures he knew as a youth. In that solitary wilderness, David the boy had come to truly know God.

Enemies do not hunt me, but life certainly nips at my heels. Thus, I especially relish the wilderness moments You offer when I can almost hear You say, "Pause and be with me." My eyes feast on silent snowfalls before the plows mar the quiet. At daybreak, I feel like the sole witness to the slowly growing glow of the rising sun. The crackle of the logs in the fireplace, the aroma of good things in the oven, or the cat purring warm and trusting in my lap transports me to a moment of solitude. Remembering to open my heart to You in these respites of calm only adds to my joy.

Because it speaks to a longing for God, Psalm 63 has been used by the faithful as a morning prayer.

Strangers

The Lord also will be a stronghold for the oppressed,
A stronghold in times of trouble;
And those who know Your name will put their trust in You,
For You, O Lord, have not forsaken those who seek You.

Psalm 9:9–10, NASB

Joyfully the faithful sing about God's wonderful attributes and deeds. In his love, he strengthens the broken and the exploited. In his faithfulness, he is the ultimate refuge for all who call upon his name. God released the Israelites from slavery and provided a homeland where they were strangers no more. No wonder they put their trust in God.

It comforts me to affirm that You know no strangers. It gives me hope to remember that in Your sight we are all Your children and family to one other. In a world of more than 7 billion people, who among us does not feel like a stranger multiple times a day? Nevertheless, You tell us to look past the skin colors and past the wrinkles of age or the glow of youth. You tell us to look at each other until we find You in every face looking back at us. You tell us no one is truly a stranger, for all of us are truly Your loves. When we can live in that belief, surely we will find joy.

"To Die for the Son," starts Psalm 9 and may refer to a song or melody known at the time.

Strength

Yahweh sat enthroned at the Flood.
Yes, Yahweh sits as King forever.
Yahweh will give strength to his people.
Yahweh will bless his people with peace.

Psalm 29:10–11, WEB

The psalmist contemplates God's power and sovereignty. He appreciates that God already was king at the time of the great flood; therefore, the power of Yahweh, the God of Israel, goes beyond time. For the Hebrews, God not only will reign forever, but also will bless and protect his chosen people through the ages. God's strength and endurance becomes theirs.

God, let's be honest here, I've never squeezed Your biceps, but I believe with the deepest joy and conviction that Your strength powers through me and my life. Oh, this body of mine won't always be strong, and I accept that my muscles will soften and be less able to lift and carry. I know I'll get slower, and likely I'll rest more, but I will not put down my load to be the best child of God I can be. Your strength will continue to move through me, boosting my moral staying power. I'm no weightlifter, but I trust every time I pray that You will pump me up and that Your daily blessing will ensure my strength.

Writers from ancient times used a worldwide flood to represent chaos, which only a mighty power like God can subdue.

Terrorism

God, don't keep silent.
Don't keep silent, and don't be still, God.

Psalm 83:1, WEB

This opening verse begins the psalmist's earnest plea to God to protect Israel from a gathering of hostile nations. These enemies are plotting against the Hebrews and are conspiring with one another to destroy those who revere God. Three times the psalmist urges God to speak up and take action on behalf of his children.

God, I know when terrorism strikes, You do not stand silent and You do not stand still. I hear Your voice in Muslims Against Terrorism, and I see You stand bravely in the NATO and UN peacekeeping forces. I see You in the countless NGOs working worldwide to educate children and to feed those weakened by famine. In the compassion of others, I see Your hands reach out to those threatened by terrorism, and I see You comfort those whom terrorists have harmed. Terrorism brings me no joy, but the work others do in Your name does. Because they believe in You, they lift the burdens of others and protect the weak even at great risk to themselves. Every day they remind me that You are with us—always.

Some scholars think Psalm 83 may have been written as a song of entreaty when Israel faced an impending assault.

Theft

For in the day of trouble he will keep me safe in his dwelling;
he will hide me in the shelter of his sacred tent
and set me high upon a rock.

Psalm 27:5, NIV

When the Israelites followed Moses into the desert, impermanent tents were their refuge against the heat and desert winds. God, however, was their refuge and their rock when their spirits and their bodies flagged. For the dispirited wandering in the deserts of their own hearts, the temple in Zion also offered refuge. There in the sanctuary, the troubled could lift themselves up onto the secure rock of faith and God's love.

God, You've taught me some important lessons about what is and what is not important in life, and You've helped me figure out what's worth my worry. So listen to my joyful shout out to the thieves of this world: You can break the lock on my door and steal my television or pinch my computer, but you can't steal what I treasure: the people I love, my trust in God, and my confidence that you are nothing more than a momentary inconvenience. You can't rob me of what I don't truly treasure; so the stuff is yours, because I know God stays with me.

In many synagogues, Psalm 27 is read during the Jewish New Year.

Time

Has his loving kindness vanished forever?
Does his promise fail for generations?
Has God forgotten to be gracious?
Has he, in anger, withheld his compassion? Selah.

Psalm 77:8–9, WEB

The psalmist wails out his fear that God has abandoned Israel. Even more terrifying is his question: Is God never coming back? In the poet's darkest hours, he imagines a life without God, and his soul sinks. A few verses later, his song will fill with the praise of someone who pauses and remembers that after the dark moments, he will find the joy of God's love.

The psalmist may be fearful God has jumped ship, but joyously I am not. I know that any fear I have that You have abandoned me has sprung from my weaknesses, not Yours. Sometimes I'm impatient, but You have plenty of time, and when I feel alone and vulnerable, it's because I haven't taken the time to hear Your voice or feel Your presence, always as close as my breath. I can pray even the sad psalms, because You have given me the great joy of knowing that at every moment in time, and through all times of trial, You are with me.

Though somber in tone, laments like Psalm 77 express a deep faith and praise for God's interventions.

Violence

You, Lord, hear the desire of the afflicted;
you encourage them, and you listen to their cry,
defending the fatherless and the oppressed,
so that mere earthly mortals will never again strike terror.

Psalm 10:17–18, NIV

The poet starts his psalm with a recurring social justice theme—the wicked seem to prosper, while the defenseless suffer at their hands. By the time he has finished his poem of worry, he reminds the prayerful to trust in God's love and protection. God not only hears the cries of the weak and the oppressed, but he also steadies their nerves so that terror will not strike their hearts.

My mind and my heart are finally at peace. The brutality that once haunted my waking life no longer terrorizes my dreams. I sleep better, I'm not as jumpy, and I don't fear the dark as much. Aggression had taken its toll on my nerves and sapped what little courage I felt to face each day, but no more. When I felt I was at a dead end, I turned to You, and that simple move saved me. Cruelty is a fierce enemy, but it no longer claims victory over me, for You are my shield and my strength.

➤ **During Rosh Hashanah, the Jewish New Year, Verse 17 is part of the Amidah, the standing prayer of the worshippers.**

War

My soul hath long dwelt
with him that hateth peace.
I am for peace:
but when I speak, they are for war.

Psalm 120:6–7, KJV

The Israelites often had to prepare for war, for their enemies were bent on their destruction. God, however, kept his promise to Abraham and ensured that Israel would become a great nation. He blessed both Israel and those who dealt fairly with God's children.

War neither blesses the world nor brings it joy, but those who follow You, God, bless the world through their dedication to peace. So, I rejoice and am joyful for the peacemakers among us who work for peaceful homes, safe neighborhoods and streets, and peaceful hearts. Peace on the local level grows peace in the world. You defended the Hebrews so they could be a blessing to their world. I trust that You will bless the citizens and nations who commit their lives to freedom from strife, not just for themselves, but also for all the peoples of the earth. Help me to be a bearer of peace in this world, so that I, in turn, can bring others joy.

Psalm 120 is the first of the fifteen psalms known as the Songs of Ascents.

Work

He trains my hands for battle,
So that my arms can bend a bow of bronze.
You have also given me the shield of Your salvation,
And Your right hand upholds me;
And Your gentleness makes me great.

Psalm 18:34–35, NASB

David, the youth who slew Goliath, became David the warrior king, whose mighty arm and battle cunning came from God. Like a battle shield, God protected him from the aggressors' flying arrows. The poet also knows that God's salvation on the battlefield followed the king into life and infused the Hebrew ruler with a gentle spirit.

I'm happy that work in my life means more than simply going to a job. When people inquire, "What do you do?" I know what they're asking; but in my heart, I know I'm busy working at more than just what earns my paycheck. I know You have thousands of job openings at feeding stations, hospitals, animal shelters, and right in my own neighborhood. Some of those assignments are in tough places, but I know You wouldn't give me a job too big to handle. I'm happy to be on Your payroll and enrolled in Your benefit plan, because a job well done means I've put my faith into action working for You.

This royal thanksgiving psalm, which some believe David wrote, retells the king's story as found in 2 Samuel 22.

God be merciful unto us, and bless us;
and cause his face to shine upon us; Selah.

Psalm 67:1, KJV

The psalmist calls upon the priestly blessing God gave to Aaron, the Hebrews' first high priest. "The Lord bless thee, and keep thee. The Lord make his face shine upon thee, and be gracious unto thee. The Lord lift up his countenance upon thee, and give thee peace." (Nm 6: 24–26, KJV) The Israelites knew from experience that when God smiled on them, peace and prosperity followed.

God, You gave me the unexpected but much-needed gift of Your blessing. You smiled on this worrywart just when I most needed to have my mind and heart put at ease. You set me free from fretting and helped me put any uneasiness aside. Do I still worry at times? Yes, I do, but when anxiousness overcomes me and my imagination gets the better of me, Your wisdom shines brightly on my concerns, and they evaporate like water in the sun. When I lift my troubles to You, You exchange them for peace of mind and the joy of a light heart. I can't resist turning my face toward You and awaiting the miracle of Your smile beaming toward me.

Muslims, Jews, and some Christian groups recognize Aaron, Moses' older brother, as a prophet.

Psalm Directory

About the Author

As a cantor for many years, Judith Galas has sung the psalms weekly at Sunday worship and hopes one day to learn how to play the lyre—King David's harp—as her accompaniment.

She has taught writing and literature in fifth through tenth grades, World Religions in middle schools, and journalism to undergraduates. Retired from the full-time classroom, she now consults and conducts writing workshops for corporations. She and her family live in Lawrence, Kansas.

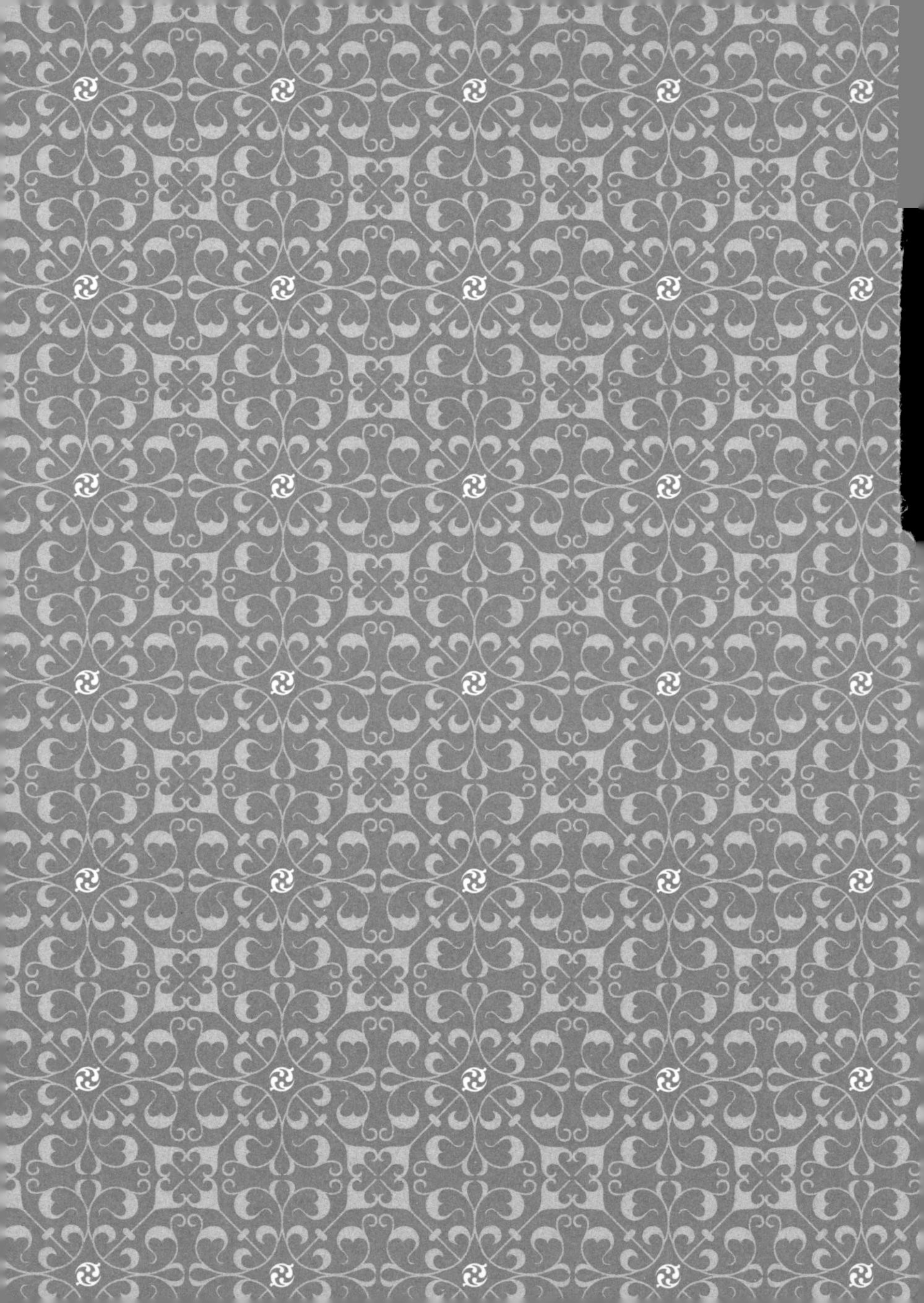